Praise for *Be Sharp*

D0932780

"In BE SHARP, Paula and Mina give you th............ solution to the crucial challenge of creating powerful, positive first impressions. In the lightning-fast pace of today's business, that first impression is quite often your one and only opening to ignite winning relationships and to seize prized opportunities. Yet, the secrets to creating and delivering dynamic personal introductions have never been adequately taught–until NOW! This clear and powerful book will do more than skyrocket your career. It will elevate your confidence and peace of mind in those crucial moments that make the biggest difference in your life."

Brian Biro - America's Breakthrough Coach

"Lots of authors are advising people to create their 'brand', but few give you detailed advice on how to approach the task. Here is the book that will help you get the ROI you want from your networking and self-marketing activities. BE SHARP gives you both the 'why' and the 'how' behind creating impactful personal introduction statements, bios, and websites. As experienced executive coaches, the authors also realize the value of producing a personal statement as a means to help you define your professional identity and 'market' the identity you want others to recognize."

Nancy Jagmin, President, Jagmin Consulting Group and
Former Vice President of Organizational Capability, Frito-Lay

"I've never seen anything like this all in one in place. This is really good! BE SHARP offers a concise formula to help any professional powerfully and appropriately let the world know who they are and what they bring to the table in a variety of different circumstances. If you are looking for a leg up on the competition - this could be it."

Chip Lambert, President, Network2Networth
Business Development for the Serious Entrepreneur

"Reading this book was like having a great conversation with Mina and Paula. It made me want to put the book down and take action immediately."

Jeff Crilley, Emmy Award Winning Journalist,
Author of Free Publicity, and Founder of Real News
Public Relations (www.realnewspr.com)

"BE SHARP is a great hands-on workbook. It is an excellent resource for mid-level executives. In particular, it would be valuable to those who have been in a single company for a number of years or those who haven't navigated the job search market recently."

Judy Stubbs, Former Partner, Heidrick & Struggles,
one of the world's foremost executive search firms,
and Former SVP HR, Mary Kay Cosmetics

"BE SHARP turns a daunting task into an easy to follow, step-by-step process that results in a clear, concise introduction for a powerful first impression."

Mike Johanns, Former Vice President, Supply Chain at Dell
and its subsidiary, Alienware, the industry leader in
gaming and high performance computing

"In BE SHARP Mina and Paula got it right. You must establish your value and make a solid first impression. In the world of retained executive search we are continually running across candidates that do not make a good first impression, and it is a short interview. If you follow their sound methodology, you will learn how to identify and articulate your value and make that all important positive first impression."

Phil Resch, Partner, Sandhurst Group

"BE SHARP fills a gap in the career management and employment literature for individuals. This book provides invaluable guidance for professionals and job seekers to help them position and market themselves more effectively in today's highly connected electronic and time-compressed world. It offers sound advice on how to write a bio that makes a good first impression in a variety of professional activities and settings – networking, websites, job fairs, employment interviews, conference presentations, consulting, training, sales, marketing, business development and press releases. The guidance in BE SHARP has been developed and tested by two seasoned executive coaches who have helped clients communicate their real strengths for business advantage. It is the definitive guide to writing a bio!"

William Banis, National Certified Career Counselor and
co-author of *High Impact Resumes and Letters*

"In BE SHARP, the authors have given us the most inventive tools I have seen to create the personal marketing materials we need in all aspects of business. The uniquely effective and efficient process takes you on a personal journey in which you will rediscover and reconnect to your most valuable talents and skills. In a few short hours, I was able to communicate my value to the marketplace with authenticity and enthusiasm."

Courtney Q. Shore, SVP, Communications and Marketing

"The book is brilliantly and concisely written relaying succinct information and interesting examples in a readable fashion. The authors' structured approach translates beautifully to capturing the essence of an individual's talents into a superb bio geared for the right market."

Mary Spilman, Managing Partner, Spilman & Associates, Inc.
Executive Search Consultants

"BE SHARP is so much more than another book about successful interviewing skills. Mina and Paula have developed a unique approach that puts you ahead of your competitors. Reading this book will give you the confidence to know that every first impression will not only be your best, but also be memorable and impressive. Can you really afford anything less?"

Anisa Aven, CEO, TurnKey Coaching Solutions

Be Sharp

"Tell Me About Yourself" in
Great Introductions and Professional Bios

First Edition: December 2008

ISBN: 1-4392-1676-2
ISBN 13: 9781439216767

DEDICATION PAGE

To Reneé, who came into my life over 20 years ago as a Big Brother Big Sister match:

You have grown into a wonderful adult. I treasure our relationship over all these years. Your outlook, your good counsel, and your adventuresome nature have added a special depth and joy to my life. Thank you.

–Paula

To my children, Michelle and Paul:

For your understanding, love and support, I am ever thankful and blessed. You both continuously teach me about the best in the human spirit through your courage, independence, resourcefulness, compassion and ageless wisdom. You inspire me. Thank you for always believing in me and making me a very proud mother.

–Mina

ACKNOWLEDGEMENTS

During the writing of this book we discovered more than ever how much our success is derived from those around us. We could never have completed this book without the support, encouragement, ideas, and creative contributions of so many special and generous people.

Our special thanks go to Lynn Asinof, for her diligent, wise, and impeccable editing; Marjie Price, for her creative flare and amazing patience in the design and creation of the cover and layout; Mabry Morrison, for making the publishing of the book happen; and to Jeff Crilley, whose inspiration, support, and encouragement were instrumental in getting us started and kept us motivated and on track throughout the process. To each of you, we deeply appreciate your gifts.

The genesis of this book came from our personal, one-on-one engagements with clients. All of the samples and examples used in this book are based on the real life experiences our clients have shared with us and the results of our work with them to create powerful documents and introductions. Of course, the names and other identifying information have been changed to maintain confidentiality. We are grateful to each and every one of you for your part in the evolution of our thinking and the development of our model. You continue to bring to light how critically important this information is. You know who you are, and we truly thank you.

Finally, writing and publishing a book is a long and sometime arduous process. Those special people around us, our friends, families, and colleagues, have endured the ordeal with grace and patience. We are proud to celebrate this accomplishment and want to acknowledge that we could not have done it without you. You have been holding high the light at the end of the tunnel. For this, we thank you.

$\mathcal{T}$able of Contents

Part Two: Professional Bios

Part Three: Bios in Business

Part Four: Practical and Powerful Applications

*I*NTRODUCTION

Every time you meet someone—or present yourself for the first time—you may be creating an impression so lasting that good or bad, it can be difficult to change. In today's fast moving and unforgiving business environment, these opportunities occur almost every day. It may be the new boss, the new client, or the job candidate you've been asked to interview. You may be invited to present an award or speak at a conference. Or you may be meeting a potential boss as part of the job interview process. A strong, positive impression can result in a job offer, a new client contract, or better business relations. A bad first impression can make others doubt your abilities, mistrust your motives, or see you as a liability. Susan Bixler, author of the book, *The Professional Image*, summarized it well when she wrote, "Although people should be judged by their innate worth, it is often a first impression that determines whether someone will stick around long enough to let them reveal it."

Few people have the personality and self-confidence to pull off a flawless personal introduction without any advance preparation or thought. If you spend just a few minutes preparing to put your best foot forward, however, you can change the way the world sees you.

As corporate leaders and professional coaches, we have rarely encountered a client who initially responded to the request "Tell me about yourself" with professional polish and pizzazz. About half start by telling some version of their life story, others just ramble in a stream of consciousness sort of way, and the rest appear to go into a trance—the "deer in headlights" look.

Yet this is one challenge that you will face over and over again in your personal and professional life. During the fall of 2006, we surveyed HR executives, managers and recruiters at two separate HR-related conferences. Recognizing the importance of first impressions, we wanted to better understand the way managers form their impressions of job candidates. We then conducted a separate survey of people who had been interviewed in the prior 12 months. Both surveys were designed to rank the frequency of specific interview questions.

In our survey, 67% of HR executives and directors said that they frequently asked candidates to "Tell me about yourself". The results were similar for recruiters who completed the survey. Moreover, 54% of all respondents in our first survey said that this is the first question they ask potential candidates.

In our survey of individuals who had been interviewed, participants overwhelmingly reported that two questions are asked more often than any other: "Why are you interested in this job?" and "Would you tell me about yourself?"

Over the years, we have found that it is common practice for executive search consultants to first ask "Would you tell me about yourself?" and then have the candidate spend the next one to two hours elaborating on their answer. These are expert interviewers who have learned that they can get the information they need by using that initial answer as the starting point for follow-up questions.

In fact, "Tell me about yourself" shows up in a variety of forms. Even if the opening question is something like, "What makes you a good candidate for this job?", your answer should be essentially the same, but modified slightly to reflect the specific form of the question. They are really asking for you to tell them about you.

What Are They Really Asking?

Tell me about your background. = Tell me about yourself.

Why should we hire you? = Tell me about yourself.

Summarize your experience. = Tell me about yourself.

Give me the highlights of your career. = Tell me about yourself.

Why don't you walk me through your job history? = Tell me about yourself.

What makes you a good candidate for this job? = Tell me about yourself.

What expertise do you bring to the team? = Tell me about yourself.

What do you feel are your best assets? = Tell me about yourself.

Why are you interested in this job? = Tell me about yourself.

We think it's clear that those who fail to develop a polished and professional answer to that critical question are doing themselves a serious disservice. Still, this is such a common deficiency among otherwise outstanding professionals that we decided to address the problem by writing this book. It is designed both to help people navigate the job search process and to apply their skill at managing first impressions to other aspects of their life.

New managers, for example, set the tone for future relationships when they introduce themselves to their teams, but they often don't take advantage of the opportunity. Students want to know that they are studying under an accomplished educator, but teachers rarely do a good job of introducing themselves. And sales professionals sometimes focus solely on their product or service, neglecting to establish their personal credibility with the customer—a factor that can adversely impact the sale.

Clients who have worked with us on their Introductions and Bios have come to see firsthand the power of first impressions. We frequently hear clients say that as a result of our training they can talk to people with new confidence and authority. They report that they are now more self-assured and that more people are listening to them. At a very personal level, too, many have been surprised by the level of insight and understanding the actual process has provided them. Clients appreciate the new-found perspective that comes from focusing on their own unique and special qualities.

We have developed a clear methodology and easy-to-use tools that can help anyone develop their own unique introduction. It is an easy step from there to writing a professional bio and a compelling resume. By helping you understand the importance of that opening statement—"Tell me about yourself"—we hope to empower you in all your business and personal interactions.

A Look Inside

Part I. Personal Introductions. Learn how to respond to "Tell me about yourself" with confidence and polish. It's not obvious to most people how to do this, so we have created an easy formula for nailing this every time in every situation.

Part II. Professional Bios. Most professionals should have something written that tells their story in a concise and targeted way. That document, your bio, needs to be engaging and attractive. You are presenting who you are and along with your entire career in one easy-to-read page. We will walk you through the process from top to bottom.

Part III. Bios in Business. A bio is not a bio is not a bio. There are numerous situations where you need a bio that is constructed in some unique way. Here you will find several of the most common business circumstances where a bio is needed. For each situation, you will learn how to take your Foundation Bio and morph it into an appropriate customized version.

Part IV. Practical and Powerful Applications. Once you have created your Introduction and your Bio, you will find that they take on a life of their own. Applications range from your web presence to coaching your staff to marketing your business. Here, we address these relevant and useful applications.

Part One

Personal Introductions

$\mathcal{H}$OW WOULD YOU INTRODUCE YOURSELF?

Robert's Story: The $100 Million Deal

Robert is up for promotion to partner with a top-tier Midwest investment banking firm. He has all the right credentials—an undergraduate degree from the University of Michigan and an MBA from the University of Pennsylvania's Wharton School. He has an easy going personality and an uncanny ability to negotiate profitable deals. His deal sheet is the envy of many of his colleagues.

Recently, Robert's boss asked him to attend a meeting with a powerful investor that the bank is soliciting for new business. This is Robert's chance to secure an important new international client, which would virtually guarantee him a promotion and large bonus payout.

Robert's boss opens the meeting with introductions around the table. It is then Robert's turn to talk about himself, his background, and the value he would add to the account. But Robert freezes. After a full minute of dead silence, he fumbles his way through a short biography. When he finally finishes, he notices the glazed look in his colleagues' eyes. "Wow. They are obviously underwhelmed," he thinks. "I can convince people from all over the world to choose our firm and close multi-million dollar deals, but I can't talk about myself for 60 seconds."

After the meeting, the boss turns and asks, "What happened to you? You may be the best person for this account, but they certainly don't know it after that!"

Sylvia's Story: The Interviewer's Dilemma

Sylvia has to find the right candidate to fill a high-profile job in her department. The person who previously held the job just got a terrific promotion to another division. Sylvia has the reputation for bringing in the company's best talent and has already interviewed six technically qualified people this week. Her interviews typically begin with "Tell me about yourself..." She calls Henrietta, the company recruiting manager and laments, "I don't know if I can do another one of these interviews. These people don't know how to present themselves so that I will want to hire them. I'm so turned off in the first two minutes that I lose interest."

Any one of the candidates interviewed probably could do the job, but one of the requirements of this position is communication with executives throughout the organization. Sylvia worries about giving any of them the job since they can't handle a basic introduction.

CHAPTER 2

WHY IS THIS SO HARD?

Despite the number of programs that now train people to create their "30-second elevator pitch", most of the pitches we hear today are just plain awful. They are awkward, boring, irrelevant, too long, too short, cliché-ridden, stiff, rehearsed, and humorless. Once in a while, someone will introduce himself or herself the "right" way, and we always remember that person. You probably do too.

You may think that honing a good introduction is simply a job interview skill, but what about meeting a new client, presenting yourself to a new team, or networking at industry events, community activities, and dinner parties. You may be an award nominee or honoree. Or you may be asked to be a guest speaker, to serve as a seminar leader, or to meet your boss's boss. And then there's the first time you introduce yourself to your prospective in-laws. As you can see, a good introduction is important any time you need to establish a connection with someone else quickly.

What keeps you from introducing yourself with ease and confidence?

Why Is Introducing Yourself So Hard?
Check all that apply.

- ❑ I believe it's impolite to brag.
- ❑ I don't know what to say.
- ❑ I'm embarrassed to talk about myself.
- ❑ I feel insincere.
- ❑ I'm afraid that people will judge me.
- ❑ I'm shy.
- ❑ No matter how much I prepare, I don't seem to be ready.

- ❑ I don't think I'm personally worthy.
- ❑ It's none of their business.
- ❑ I'm not confident enough to put myself in the limelight.
- ❑ It feels superficial.
- ❑ The other person really doesn't want to know about me.
- ❑ It's too personal.
- ❑ In my culture, it is inappropriate for people to talk about themselves.

Cultural Bias

Every culture has its own view of what is considered polite. Most modern cultures, however, frown on people who talk continuously about their own accomplishments.   While it is okay for someone else to describe you in glowing terms, it is generally considered impolite to say the same things about yourself. In this book, we will explain how you can talk deftly about yourself without appearing to brag.

Emotional Resistance

Fear of being judged is one of the most common reasons for poor personal introductions.   People tend to be far more aware of their weaknesses than they are of their strengths. Indeed, many people have such high expectations for themselves that they have a hard time focusing on what they do well. What if you were to ask someone else what your strengths or talents are? What would they say?

Learning how to pitch yourself is empowering. The very act of crafting your own introduction produces a sense of accomplishment and a higher level of self-esteem. Using our methodology, our clients often respond to their new introductions saying "Wow, is that really me? I like that person. I'd like to meet that person." Or even better, they say, "I'd like to interview that person."

Assumptions

We make assumptions every day, usually without stopping to think about their veracity. Often, these assumptions turn out to be self-defeating. When we are asked to describe ourselves, for example, it is easy to assume that people aren't really interested. We may think that they are just making conversation. Or we might assume that our answer will sound superficial or insincere. Done poorly, it actually may be superficial and insincere. Learning how to introduce yourself in any setting is an important statement about you.

Common Introduction Mistakes
Have you heard these?

1. **Life chronology:** *I was born in ..., and raised in ... I went to college at ... My first job was... I'm married and have two kids and two dogs.*

2. **Totally personal approach:** *I'm very organized. I'm an early morning person, and my hobbies include bird watching and badminton.*

3. **Just jobs:** *I am the vice president of ... at ... company. I am responsible for eight direct reports and an organization of 100 people. We manufacture widgets that are sold to ... I conduct weekly staff meetings at 8 a.m. on Mondays and quarterly all hands meetings. Prior to this job, I was the Director of ... at ... etc., etc., etc.*

4. **Inappropriate information:** *Oh there's so much to tell. Where do I start? I just moved into our new 3,000 square foot house, and we had so much trouble getting the TIVO installed. I finally feel like I have my head above water, and I'm ready for work.*

A good introduction must be not only factually accurate, but it must also come from the heart.

Skills

Most people would admit that they don't know how to properly respond to "Tell me about yourself". That's because most people have no model for developing a good introduction. No one has ever provided them with guidelines about what to say, what not to say, and how much information to provide. This book will provide you with a simple, straightforward model for crafting an introduction that you can use effectively for the rest of your career and the rest of your life.

CHAPTER 3

PRESCRIPTION FOR A POLISHED INTRODUCTION

Too many people answer the question "Would you tell me about yourself?" by taking a literal approach. But the query might actually be better understood as "Who are you?" Thus the right answer isn't to provide a biography, a listing of all your prior jobs, or a catalogue of your interests and hobbies. Instead, you need a simple summary of who you are. To sum up your unique talents, your experience and your personal style, you need to address the following three "factors."

 The Essence Factor: This is the summation of who you are in one sentence. What "file folder" do you belong in?

 The Guru Factor: This let's people know what you know. What special expertise do you have?

 The Star Factor: These are the things that set you apart. Beyond your knowledge, what do people admire about you?

In the next three chapters, we will explore each of these factors in depth. Then we will help you to create your own Essence, Guru, and Star Factors so that you can use them to create your Personal Introduction.

Just the Facts

To do that, however, you will have to address those cultural, emotional and psychological barriers that make it so hard to craft an effective introduction. A good approach is to shift your perspective so that you focus on the facts—just the facts.

Despite what you may think, describing yourself is not personal. It's factual. You need to get comfortable with being able to talk about yourself in a neutral, non-emotional way.   Here are two important concepts that will help.

Be specific: When speaking of yourself, provide sufficient information so that your audience will conclude you are exceptional.   How do you do that? You need to drill down to the specifics. For example, if you are "smart", what does that really mean? Are you someone who sees solutions quicker than others, or are you someone who is really good at defining problems. Are you academically smart or street-smart, or both?

Use someone else's words: This is a remarkably effective way of providing such information. Instead of describing your outstanding characteristics in the first person (I am . . .), you can draw on statements that others have made or would make about you.   For example, rather than stating, "I am an exceptional CIO", John can say "The CFO recently described me as an exceptional CIO." That's a fair statement and far more comfortable to say. And since it was exactly what the CFO said, it's also factual.

Finally, remember that every person brings something special to the table. It's simply a matter of paying attention and allowing yourself to recognize your own talents and accomplishments. No two people are alike, so focus on your unique qualities.

CHAPTER 4

γOUR ESSENCE FACTOR

You are at a meeting, seated at a table with a half-dozen other people who are introducing themselves using no more than three or four words such as facilities manager, aerospace engineer, or CFO. What three or four words would you use to describe yourself?

Rather than simply choosing the job you hold today, take a broader perspective. Think about your career, the job you held before this one, and the job that will come next. What words capture your essential qualities as a professional? These words are the core of your "Essence Factor".

> **Step 1:**
> Jot down 3-4 words that you would use to describe your essential qualities as a professional.

They should be designed to help people understand you clearly and quickly. Picture this: if you were sorting people into file drawers, you might put the engineers into one "drawer", the accountants into another "drawer", and the airplane pilots into a third. This label will allow people to figure out how to "file you". It's as simple as that.

Next, find a modifier that you can put in front of those descriptor words. That modifier should convey a strong, dynamic aspect of your abilities. Jot down three or four possible choices that would strengthen your description. Choose the modifer you like best.

> **Step 2:**
> Add a strong modifier that describes a defining dynamic quality about you.

Think of this as a powerful stake in the ground that establishes your first impression.   Remember, it also needs to stand alone in those few instances when this is all you are allowed to say.

Step 3:
Create a sentence by adding more specifics about who you are.

Now let's assume everyone at the table can introduce themselves with a whole sentence. What would you want to add that gives people a better picture of who you are?   It might be something about your industry or an area of your background or a functional specialty.   For example, if you are currently a senior financial executive, you might want to tell people that you have public accounting experience or hail from Wall Street. If you are an IT person, you might want to say that you specialize in the oil and gas industry.

Here are some examples of good first sentences.

- Hello. I'm **Leroy Williams**, and I'm a business analyst in operations and a technology-savvy project manager.

- IIi, there. My namc is **Nicole Sherrod**. I am a consulting partner in the Consumer Products practice of Bearing & Loitte.

- Good morning.   My name is **Shana Milner**.   I'm a business strategist with strong financial and IT experience now working as an operations executive at Med Supply Corporation.

There is an alternative "salesy" approach to introductions that is in vogue these days. It is used primarily in face-to-face interactions, such as networking events or informal situations.

Here are a couple of examples:

- Certified financial planner: "I help people realize their dreams."

- Life coach: "Whatever is happening in your life that you want to change—I can help."

This approach can be effective in certain circumstances, creating a unique introduction. However, it can also backfire, turning off some listeners. So be careful, it's not for everyone. We have also found that this approach can put the "cart before the horse" since you begin your introduction without giving a proper framework for the information.

Nonetheless, it might be worthwhile for you to construct your own version of this approach and experiment with it. Remember, this kind of introduction has limited application and cannot be used in every situation. It is definitely not appropriate for interviews, formal sales presentations, and most written introductions or bios.

Be Memorable

1. Introductions need to be memorable. When you are at networking events or informal social settings where people don't know you, you want to make your name stick. It is your responsibility for others to remember who you are, including your name. Is there anything unique about your name? Use it. If you have a more common name, link it to something that is in the news, is connected with the entertainment industry, or will make a connection with your audience. Finally, in a formal networking introduction, remember to repeat your name at the end.

2. A good introduction is not boring. Use colorful or powerful adjectives that give you personality.

3. What you choose to talk about here must be carefully selected to highlight what matters for your purpose. Don't include something that diverts attention away from your goals.

Your ESSENCE FACTOR Worksheet

Step 1: Jot down 3-4 words that you would use to describe your essential qualities as a professional.

_____

_____

_____

Step 2: Add a strong modifier that describes a defining dynamic quality about you.

_____

_____

_____

Step 3: Create a sentence by adding more specifics about who you are.

_____

_____

_____

_____

CHAPTER 5

YOUR GURU FACTOR

Most accomplished people have developed a specific knowledge base upon which they have built their careers. This knowledge base is the foundation of their "Guru Factor". It's the knowledge that they have that sets them apart from everyone else. To figure out your own Guru Factor, think about the kinds of things people ask you when they want your knowledge. For example, if you are a financial person, do they turn to you when they want to know more about SEC reporting or International Financial Reporting Standards (IFRS)? If you are an IT person, you may know more about testing than others.

Step 4:
List all your special areas of knowledge.

Make a list of all your areas of expertise. Start with the statement "I have expertise in or in-depth knowledge of ..." Then consider the possibilities. What do you study? What are your passions? When others research those areas, do they call you? Do you have a lot of technical knowledge or a deep level of understanding in a particular area or subject?

Once you have a list, select the top one or two areas of expertise. What are those areas where you are the "go-to" person in your organization? Most people will find that they have one or two areas that truly set them apart.

Step 5:
Select your top one or two that are relevant to your goals.

Some people, however, find it tough to identify their Guru Factor. If you can't identify one or two areas of expertise, move on to your Star Factor. People who lack a strong Guru Factor will often have a large number of Star Factors, which can also serve as a strong base for a successful career.

Once you have established your Guru Factor, you need to elaborate by creating a "key word" sentence. There may be areas of expertise that you take for granted but nonetheless differentiate you from others. This sentence provides a context for your expertise. It might look like this: "I have expertise in SEC reporting as well as in-depth knowledge of current strategic planning methodologies."

Step 6:
Create a sentence that clearly communicates your expertise.

You met Leroy, Nicole and Shana in Chapter 4. Here are the Guru Factors that they might have constructed:

- **Leroy**: I have expertise in business systems development for database marketing services, including structuring and managing the data for these applications.

- **Nicole**: After several years crisscrossing the globe, I am known around the world for providing expertise in Six-Sigma principles as they are applied to factory-floor processes.

- **Shana**: I have in-depth knowledge of global supply chain and enterprise systems.

Be Clear

1. Your Guru Factor is about what you KNOW, not what you DO. It addresses your knowledge base, not how you get things done.
2. Not every person will have a Guru Factor. If you don't, leave it out. Increase your emphasis on your Star Factor. Someone who is a "jack of all trades and master of none" may be able to lead teams, mediate problems, or otherwise be very successful in how they do things.

Your GURU FACTOR Worksheet

Step 4: List all your special areas of knowledge.

_____

_____

_____

_____

_____

Step 5: Select your top one or two that are relevant to your goals.

_____

_____

_____

Step 6: Create a sentence that clearly communicates your expertise.

_____

_____

_____

_____

CHAPTER 6

YOUR STAR FACTOR

 What things do you do that set you apart as a star? To answer that question, use your peer group, however you define it, as your point of reference. These are the people you compete with every day and against whom you will be compared. Think about your Star Factor in the context of how you get things done. It is often about your personal qualities, professional characteristics, and style and how those elements are applied in your work life. Sometimes this is an opportunity to talk about your "soft" skills.

Step 7:
Create a list of qualities and attributes that others see in you that set you apart from your peers.

Once again, it is important to be specific. What exactly makes you a star? If you find yourself struggling with this, think about what other people have said about you.

As with the Guru Factor, start by making a thorough list of all these characteristics. Consider which ones work well with your other factors, which ones position you best with your audience, and which ones are most closely aligned with your goals. Select the top few.

Step 8:
Select the few that are outstanding, most important to your success, and consistent with your focus.

Here are some provocative questions that might help you identify these elements.

- What positive things did your boss say in your last performance review?

- What have your customers said about you? Why do they buy from you?

- Why did you receive that award?

- Why do people want to work with or for you?

- Why would a former boss rehire or recruit you?

- What do people count on you for?

Step 9:
For those few, expand the description to show why it matters.

Now, elaborate on each of these top elements. Create a compelling description about how you work and what difference it makes. Answer these questions:

- Why is it important?

- Why does anybody care?

- What difference does it make?

- How does that play out in your job?

- Why does it matter?

Step 10:
Create the sentences that showcase your distinguishing capabilities.

The "Star Factor" part of your introduction generally begins with the words "recognized for . . .", "distinguished by . . .", "known for . . .", or "others say . . .". The "others" in this case are customers, clients, bosses, coworkers, employees, and colleagues. Your Star Factor will most likely be structured in two sentences. Here are some examples for Leroy, Nicole and Shana:

Leroy: Because I anticipate problems and identify opportunities early in a project, I have a proven track record of bringing in mission-critical projects on time. I am also known for helping to establish an understanding of our technology with end-users.

Nicole: Clients rely on my advice because of the time I've spent in the field working directly with their employees at plant locations.

Shana: As a person who really "gets" the company vision, I'm the one who is usually asked to lead complex change initiatives.

Be Specific

1. Try to avoid generic business words like "leadership skills" or "communication ability". They are too broad to be descriptive. What exactly do you do that makes you a great leader or outstanding communicator? It is the specifics that set you apart from all the other great leaders and outstanding communicators.

2. Remember that your Star Factor is incomplete without the supporting component about why it matters. Just having integrity is a good thing, but lots of people have integrity. What difference does it make in executing your responsibilities? You are a great team builder. So what? A lot of people are smart. What makes your intelligence useful? "Bob's insight into evolving technology makes him invaluable in turning product designs into market winners."

Your STAR FACTOR Worksheet

Step 7: Create a list of qualities and attributes that other see in you that set you apart from your peers.

_____

_____

_____

_____

_____

_____

_____

Step 8: Select the few that are outstanding, most important to your success, and consistent with your focus.

_____

_____

_____

_____

_____

_____

_____

_____

Step 9: For those few, expand the description to show why it matters.

_____

_____

_____

_____

_____

_____

_____

_____

Step 10: Create the sentences that showcase your distinguishing capabilities.

_____

_____

_____

_____

_____

_____

_____

_____

$\mathcal{P}$UTTING IT ALL TOGETHER

Take all these sentences—your Essence, Guru, and Star Factors—and use them to write a paragraph. Use simple, uncomplicated sentences. Use active voice. Make it short and sweet, easy to remember, and catchy. Make sure that it flows. So now, tell me about yourself!

Talk It

Once you have written your introduction, ask yourself, "Will I be comfortable saying what I've written?" If not, change it. Make it work for you. Now say it out loud. Make sure that you can comfortably "talk" it. It may seem wonderful on paper but be very difficult to deliver orally.

Here are personal introductions developed by taking the Factors for Leroy, Nicole and Shana, putting them together, and refining them for "talkability". Imagine these people are introducing themselves to you.

- Hello. I'm **Leroy Williams**, and I'm a business analyst in operations and a technology-savvy project manager. I

Catchy?

Here are some sample sentences that we consider "catchy".

- Although I have an undergraduate degree in engineering, I was recruited by Technology Inc. into Sales and Marketing, and I've never looked back.

- Hi. My name is Jenny Jerome, and I'm the CIO of Monteforte Service. Believe it or not, I'm a master gamer.

What could you do with yours to make it more interesting and catchy?

have expertise in systems development for database marketing services. I bring in mission-critical projects on time because I anticipate problems early and get 'em fixed. My end users love me because I help them understand our technology.

☞ Hi, there. My name is **Nicole Sherrod**. I am a consulting partner in the Consumer Products practice of Bearing & Loitte. I've been traveling around the world bringing Six-Sigma to our clients' factories. My clients trust my advice because I've spent so much time in the field working directly with their employees.

☞ Good morning. My name is **Shana Milner**, vice president at Med Supply Corporation. I'm a business strategist with strong background in finance and IT. I have in-depth knowledge of global supply chain and enterprise systems. I'm often asked to lead large change initiatives because I understand all the moving pieces in making change successful.

Notice how these introductions have changed slightly when refined for "talkability". Note that their sentences are short, simple, and easier to say.

Write it.

Talk it.

Test it.

The key here is to craft something that sums you up quickly, clearly and professionally. Once that message is clear, make sure you practice, practice, practice. This brief introduction should be so well rehearsed that it doesn't sound rehearsed. You need to be able to display confidence, humor, and positive energy.

Remember, your introduction will always be a work in progress. It will evolve depending on who you are talking to, what your goals are, and how your career develops.

Test It

Once you have practiced your Personal Introduction alone, try it out on someone else. Remember, effective communication is like a dance. It has a rhythm and flow. When you are giving your Personal Introduction, you need to establish rapport with your audience. If you are paying attention, you can read the responses of your listeners.

Ask for honest feedback and don't settle for easy answers. If you just ask people how they like it, they could easily say, "It's fine." This is not helpful.

If you give them specific criteria for judging, they can give you feedback that is helpful.

To assist you in gathering meaningful feedback, we've created a Personal Introduction Feedback Form that is included at the end of this chapter. It will help you get honest and useful opinions from your listeners.

Networking or Job Search "Elevator Pitch"

In various situations including a job search or networking for business development, you may be attending networking events where you have the opportunity to stand up and introduce yourself. This is commonly known as your 30 second elevator pitch. The only difference between this and your Personal Introduction is the addition of a sentence or two at the end that summarizes what you want or how someone can help you. Tell the group something specific that they can do to assist you. For example, in a job search, you may be looking for an introduction into the finance department at a particular company. In a business networking setting, you may want introductions to prospective customers, such as someone who is recently retired and may need to roll over their 401(k).

30 seconds really means 30 seconds— not 3 minutes!

Once you have delivered your pitch, it is helpful to repeat your name (and company if applicable) again at the very end along with an easy way for them to contact you. This could be your website. This helps people remember you, which after all is the point of the meeting!

Until you feel completely comfortable and secure with your pitch, we recommend that you write it out, print it, and drop it into your briefcase or portfolio. That way you can review and practice it on the way to networking events to ensure that it is fresh, polished, and top of mind.

From Introduction to Positioning

Your written Personal Introduction forms the basis for your Positioning that is used in both your bio and your resume. Having a clear Positioning is the cornerstone of your personal "marketing kit". It carries your message consistently throughout all your communication, written and oral. It is your branding, and you want it to be strong and memorable. Later in this book, you will be using your Positioning to create your Professional Bio.

People should see and hear your message over and over again. You have a multitude of opportunities to practice your pitch and get the word out. Use them.

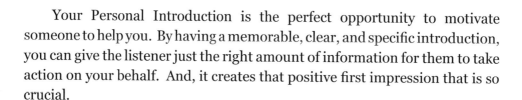

Be Compelling

Your Personal Introduction is the perfect opportunity to motivate someone to help you. By having a memorable, clear, and specific introduction, you can give the listener just the right amount of information for them to take action on your behalf. And, it creates that positive first impression that is so crucial.

Be Sharp!

Be Memorable.

Be Clear.

Be Specific.

Be Compelling.

Your PERSONAL INTRODUCTION Worksheet

Step 11: Write your first draft by putting all your Factors together.

_____

_____

_____

_____

_____

_____

_____

_____

_____

Step 12: Say it out loud and edit your Introduction for "talkability".

_____

_____

_____

_____

_____

_____

_____

_____

PERSONAL INTRODUCTION Feedback Form

Would you be willing to listen to my Personal Introduction and give me your honest evaluation? Here are some questions I would like you to consider as you listen.

Yes	No	QUESTION	WHAT IT MEANS
		Is it clear?	Do you immediately get a picture of the person being described?
		Is it me?	Do you recognize me, the person you know?
		Is it engaging?	Does it portray me as a person with distinguishing and valuable capabilities and qualities?
		Is it memorable?	Is it catchy and interesting to listen to? Would you remember me?
		Does it have impact?	Does it have a WOW factor? Does it showcase my talents?
		Does it capture the essence of my story?	Does it flow easily into more detail?
		Was it delivered well?	Did I come across as comfortable and authentic?

Part Two

Professional Bios

CHAPTER 8

WHY DO I NEED A BIO?

Now that you can respond to "Tell me about yourself" in a short paragraph, you may find you that you sometimes need a more detailed answer. That's the role of a professional bio. It puts flesh on the bare bones of your Introduction. A professional bio is your personal marketing tool and is particularly valuable for job searches. Its purpose is to help you sell YOU to networking contacts, to prospective employers and to the market in general. Yes, you have a resume. But that resume serves a different purpose, providing a factual chronology rather than a narrative. The bio, on the other hand, allows to you tell your story, making it short, sweet, and engaging.

Your bio is like your personal press release. It should entice someone to want to get to know you or, even better, to interview you. Once someone understands your story—which is not a summary of your life experience—he or she can use the resume to fill in the details. The bio gives the reader guidance in understanding how to think about you. The resume provides the details. Here's a chart that compares the characteristics of a resume with those of a bio.

Resume	Bio
Announces to the world that you're looking for a job	Applicable to almost any situation so that it's safe to be public—no unwanted exposure or jeopardy
It's about details—provides relevant facts about your work history, accomplishments, and credentials	It's about spin—cherry picks your most outstanding characteristics and accomplishments
Must be scannable but is more compressed and often not read in detail; hard to differentiate what's important and to communicate the real story line	Short, easily readable, absorbed quickly by the reader
Two pages, single spaced, small point size	One page, 1.5 or double spaced, larger font, generally less than 300 words
Job search tool in two possible venues (internal or external)	Multi-purpose document that can be used in a wide variety of venues
Almost anyone has a resume	Usually bios are associated with only senior professionals and executives
Resume development helps you get control of the details of your experience and refreshes your memory about your capabilities and accomplishments	Bio development is a uniquely powerful process for learning how to present yourself in person as well as in writing

Bio and Resume—an Example of Each

What do those differences look like on paper? Consider the following examples. The first is a bio for a senior financial executive. The second document is the same person's resume.

Sample Matching Bio

John Mendoza, CPA

Corporate Controller & Corporate Officer
American Corporation

Global Manufacturing — Strategy - M&A — Risk Management — Technology

John Mendoza is an innovative and strategic senior financial executive. He has extensive financial expertise in strategic investments and operational projects, primarily in the U.S. and Latin American markets. He is often called on to lead complex strategic initiatives to leverage a broad experience base, a consultative communication style, and a proven track record in managing project management skills. John has a unique capability to counsel operational teams to better focus operation and market strategies and to provide intuitive insight to the board of directors and executive management team to develop sound business and financial strategies. John is also integrally involved in determining investor communication strategy and managing the analyst call process.

Currently, as Corporate Controller and Corporate Officer for American Corporation, a publicly held global manufacturer and distributor of specialty materials, John manages all financial operations worldwide, including the financial aspects of M&A initiatives. In this role, he led the team that successfully established a $50 million manufacturing campus in Mexico - from Board approval through the start up. He also helped generate over $6.5 million in productivity gains by playing a key role in the successful launch of Six Sigma and by streamlining consolidated reporting systems.

Previously, as Division Controller at Maximum Industries, he drove $1 million in savings from headcount reduction and system rationalizations in leading a reorganization of the finance team. He also served as a Senior Audit Manager where he reduced the audit budget over $500,000 by redirecting focus to business risk and developing more efficient audit tools. He began his career at GMPK International where he rose to the position of Audit Manager. While at GMPK, he spent two years in Mexico City, where he gained financial reporting expertise in Latin American business environments.

John is a CPA. He holds a BBA, Magna Cum Laude, from the University of South Florida and a MS in Accounting from the University of Florida.

4221 Marketplace Road, Milwaukee, WI 09999
444-555-1234 (home) • 444-666-9876 (cell) • john.mendoza@email.com

Sample Traditional Resume

JOHN MENDOZA, CPA
john.mendoza@email.com

4221 Marketplace Road
Milwaukee, WI 09999

Cell: (444) 666-9876
Home: (444) 555-1234

Senior Financial Executive
Manufacturing and Distribution

Innovative and strategic financial leader with a Big 4 public accounting background. Extensive expertise in strategic investments and operational projects, primarily in the U.S. and Latin American markets. Often called on to lead complex strategic initiatives to leverage a broad experience base, a consultative communication style, and a proven track record in managing project management skills. Known for developing strong teams. Passion for making the most out of every opportunity, which inspires others to strive for and deliver exceptional results.

Global - Strategy - M&A - Risk Management - Technology

EXPERIENCE

AMERICAN CORPORATION (NYSE:ACO)   www.amcorp.com   2001 - Present
$350 million dollar, global manufacturer and distributor of specialty polymer composite materials and components to growing markets around the world. Products are based on core technologies in polymers, fillers and adhesion

Corporate Controller - Corporate Officer, Milwaukee, WI
Manage all public and internal financial and operational reporting, strategic planning and capital administration, financial system implementations and administration, M&A, operation initiatives, and financial service functions. Direct management of 25 corporate finance staff and oversight of over 50 worldwide operational finance professionals.

- Led the successful acquisition and integration of multiple companies ranging from $15 to $85 million in annual revenues. Also led the divestiture of a $35 million non-strategic business and the start up of an India-based $25 million joint venture.
- Led the team that successfully established a $50 million manufacturing and distribution center in Mexico - from Board approval through the start up of operations.
- Eliminated over $1.5 million in corporate overhead through streamlining of consolidated reporting systems and processes and improving quality (accuracy, integrity, timeliness) of the executive financial and operational reporting model.
- Generated over $5 million in productivity gains by playing a key role in the successful launch of Six Sigma within the organization.

MAXIMUM INDUSTRIES (NYSE:MSM)   www.maximumind.com   1998 - 2001
$4 billion dollar company that manufactures and sells a wide range of products through its electrical and tools businesses

Division Controller - Tools Division, Los Angeles, CA (1999-2001)
Managed all financial and tax reporting, financial analysis, budget and capital administration, treasury, financial support functions, and internal control administration for the $950 million Tools Division. Direct management of 25 division financial staff and oversight of 200 financial staff within the division operations.
- Drove $1 million in savings from headcount reduction, process streamlining, and system rationalization in leading the reorganization as the company consolidated two divisions.
- Completed numerous multi-million dollar strategic initiatives by providing financial project management in acquisitions and integration, operational restructuring, and asset dispositions.

Corporate Audit, Senior Manager, Chicago, IL (1998-1999)
Teamed with management in identifying critical business risks and developing innovative business solutions including new ERP system implementations, major joint venture investments in Brazil, new acquisitions, plant expansions/rationalizations, and Corporate reporting.
- Reduced audit budget by over $500,000 by redirecting focus to business risk and developed new assurance service tools to deploy the new business risk philosophy.
- Instrumental in the $7 million reduction of the purchase price of a major acquisition through due diligence and careful evaluation of market conditions.

GMPK INTERNATIONAL   www.gmpk.com   1991 - 1998
Largest global public accounting firm

Audit Manager, Miami, FL (1997-1998)
Assistant Audit Manager, Mexico City, Mexico (1994-1996)
Supervising Senior Accountant, Miami, FL (1991-1994)

Managed a diverse multinational client base in manufacturing, retail and distribution including a $3 billion publicly traded, global, world-class supplier of power generation equipment and services.
- Led the office's first outsourcing of a major client's internal audit function which produced a 25% annual savings for the company and $2 million of incremental revenue for the firm.
- Established a firmwide reputation for expertise in the Mexican accounting practices and statutory reporting regulations.

EDUCATION & CERTIFICATIONS

MS Accounting, University of Florida, 1994
BBA, University of South Florida, 1990
Graduated Magna Cum Laude
CPA, State of Florida, 1991

Resume Versus Bio?

When trying to figure out when to use a bio instead of a resume, it is useful to think about yourself as a product in the process of being marketed. Consider some key marketing materials. Companies often produce beautiful 20-page glossy brochures that describe a product, its features and benefits in great detail. They also create flyers or tri-fold pamphlets that are used primarily during the first interactions with prospective customers, the purpose of which is to get customers interested. It should intrigue them enough so that they ask for more information. Most sales people will tell you that they never make a sale by leading with their 20-page glossy brochure. In a job search, your resume is the equivalent of your glossy brochure. Your bio is the equivalent of the much briefer tri-fold or flyer.

Henry's Story: Networking With Confidence

Henry is an engineering manager with 18 years of experience. He has been looking for a job for four months. With the help of an Internet career services firm, he sent out 248 resumes without receiving a single positive response. He also posted his resume on line with several job sites, but with no luck. He's naturally a little shy and doesn't feel comfortable meeting strangers. He was hoping that the resume "blast" would produce at least a few interviews. One of his friends recommended a career coach, saying that the coach had helped him the year before.

Henry made an appointment primarily because he didn't know what else to do. He was already quite anxious about his situation. During the first session, the coach asked questions about Henry's networking activities. Henry acknowledged that he wasn't doing much networking, largely because he didn't really know what to say. The coach helped Henry develop his personal introduction and his bio. The process of just creating a bio helped Henry to see himself in a more positive light. He became proud of what he had accomplished and became comfortable telling his own story.

Once he had a clear idea how to talk about himself, Henry felt more confident participating in networking activities and making connections with current and former colleagues. The bio also gave him the right kind of communication tool to use as an introduction with networking connections.

Rick's Story: Back to First Place

Rick was a fast-tracker his whole life. He was recruited for a great job right out of college and was consistently promoted. Recruiters regularly called him. In one case, he moved to a new job when a former boss recruited him. He was THE hot property throughout his career.

When the economics of his industry suddenly shifted, however, Rick was one of many highly-qualified people who lost their jobs. For the first time in his life, he found himself competing with other top performers for a very small number of jobs at his salary and experience level. In order to stand out from the pack, he needed to make a strong and positive initial impression to differentiate himself in a market flooded with excellent candidates.

After losing an important job interview opportunity to a former colleague, Rick learned that the successful candidate had used a professional bio to introduce himself. When he saw the bio, Rick found it so impressive that he understood why his friend had been selected. He was also determined that he wouldn't end up in second place again. Working with a coach to create a terrific bio, he landed both an interview and a job offer within 30 days. He later told his friend that the bio process "was one of the best things I have ever done professionally".

CHAPTER 9

$\mathcal{H}$OW DO I USE A BIO?

Paul's Story: Job Search Unannounced

Paul and his wife wanted to move to Seattle to be closer to family members, including Paul's aging parents. They also were attracted by the region's rich variety of outdoor activities. Having been a successful executive with the same major retailer for 18 years, Paul realized that such a move meant re-positioning himself in a different city. He had good contacts through his family, but none in his industry. He did, however, know people who knew people in the industry, so he asked them to help him network with his list of target companies including REI, Starbucks, Nordstrom, Microsoft, and Costco. To arm them with the right information, he sent his bio.

One of those bios found its way to an executive with a major national retailer who contacted Paul. Paul then sent a resume, which led to an invitation for an interview. Three weeks later, Paul returned to Seattle, interviewed for a job and was offered a position. The bio was the tool that paved the way for Paul's eventual relocation to Seattle.

Why didn't Paul send his resume? He had several good reasons. 1) Resumes are a public announcement that you are actively job hunting. Paul wasn't ready to make that kind of announcement. Bios don't carry the same implication as resumes. Thus, his bio could be in anyone's hands for any reason at any time. 2) A resume doesn't tell a story–it is an informational document. That means the reader would have to try to piece together Paul's story using the facts in the resume. This would be inefficient and potentially dangerous, allowing the reader to come to incorrect conclusions about his real story. By using a bio, Paul stayed in the driver's seat. 3) Paul understood that too much information diluted his message. His goal was to provide just enough information to get people interested in more dialogue and to ask for a resume.

Sally's Story: Keynote Speaker

Sally was invited to be the keynote speaker at her women's technology organization. As director of information security at a major credit card company, she was well prepared to speak on the topic, which was identity theft. She was excited by the opportunity but was a little nervous, since this would be her first such speech to an outside organization. She was surprised when the program director called and asked for a bio that could be used both for advance publicity and for her conference introduction.

Sally had never felt any need for a bio, so she didn't have one. She called the speaker from the previous month and said, "I was so impressed with your intro and bio. How did you write it?" Her friend replied, "I have a coach who helps me with things like that. I didn't know what should go in it or how long it should be. Based on the feedback I've received, apparently it was perfect! I'll be glad to give you her name."

When the presentation day arrived, the meeting was sold out. Several people said that they decided to attend because the marketing materials connected with their interest in the topic. As the president began Sally's introduction, she thought, "Wow! I really want to hear what Sally has to say."

CHAPTER 10

WHY MOST BIOS ARE BAD

Lots of bios can be found on websites, in marketing brochures, in sales presentations and in promotional press releases. Yet most of these bios are basically boring, providing little insight into the person behind the bio. These bios say "held this job, did this, held that job, did that, went to school there, grew up somewhere, married the high school sweetheart, and has 1.8 kids." Change the names and locations and that bio could be representative of about 80% of professionals in America. You may be impressed by the credentials of the people in those bios, but you aren't likely to be engaged with the people themselves.

One reason for this uniformity of style is that bios are frequently written by a third party who doesn't necessarily understand the story or the audience. They simply drop data into a predetermined format, and voilá—another bio. The person being "bio-ed" may have little or no input into the process.

> The only people who actually like those long detailed bios are headhunters who are looking for candidates. It's an easy way to compile dossiers on key prospects.

Finally, bios tend to be both too long and way too detailed, covering a person's entire career and credentials. There is just too much information. The only people who actually like those long detailed bios are headhunters looking for candidates. They see such bios as an easy resource to be used for compiling complete dossiers on key prospects.

Bios should serve a specific purpose. The content should be designed for a particular audience and to meet a clear objective. The best bios are carefully crafted to focus on the interests of that audience. Unfortunately, most bios are "all purpose" and not appropriately targeted for their intended use.

CHAPTER 11

*T*HE FOUNDATION BIO

If you are only going to have one bio, it should be a Foundation Bio. Ultimately you may need a variety of bios—a business bio for use in marketing your services, a speaker's bio to serve as an introduction, or even a special bio for use when seeking a seat on a board of directors. All of these can be derived from this single document. Think of the Foundation Bio as the starting place.

Your bio begins with your formal name in the heading. If you use a nickname, you can switch to that name for the rest of the bio. If you are known only by your nickname, you may elect to use it exclusively throughout the bio instead of your given name. In that case, start with your nickname in the heading.

Then, your heading includes your title and company or your headline. In both cases, you add key words.

The body of the Foundation Bio consists of four paragraphs.

1. Positioning
2. Current or most recent job

Nicknames

How you handle your nickname will depend on how tightly it is tied to your professional identity. If your nickname IS your professional identity, then you may use it instead of your given name or you may use it along with your given name.

> CJ Jones
>
> Charles "CJ" Jones
>
> Charles (CJ) Jones
>
> Charles ("CJ") Jones

3. The rest of your career

4. Credentials

You may deviate slightly from this template in order to best present your career and accomplishments. Contact information is provided in a "footer". Now let's get started.

Heading

The heading will depend on your current job status. If you are employed, it's simple. The heading consists of the following:

Your Name

Your Title

Your Company

If you are not currently employed, replace your title and company with a headline you fashion out of the core of your Essence Factor.

Your Name

Your Headline

Your headline is the three to four words that reflect who you are as a professional. It is not your job title. It focuses on where you are going in the future rather than where you have been in the past. It should provide a clear indication of your level of experience and your functional expertise, if relevant. Sometimes your headline will include a descriptor or adjective that increases its impact. It is not the functional descriptor of your most recent job. Think bigger! You want to tell people who you are and where you are going.

Here are some examples of good headlines:

- Global Supply Chain Executive
- Top-Performing Account Executive
- Operations-Focused CFO—Manufacturing
- Proven Project Manager
- Nationally Recognized Security Consultant
- Emerging Technology Strategist

Key Words

In most bios, the key words come immediately after your heading. Here, you are choosing those four to six things that together set you apart and define you uniquely. The process of selecting your key words starts with some brainstorming. Don't edit your thoughts until you have a long list.

Ask yourself the following questions:

- What characteristics will be of interest to this particular audience?

- What are your industry's "hot buttons"—those areas where your expertise is most likely to generate a response, perhaps due to a shortage of resources or talent?

- What do you know that few others know?

- Are there some areas of responsibility that define you particularly well?

- In a job search, what capabilities is the hiring manager looking for?

- What makes you stand out from colleagues who have jobs similar to yours?

- Are there unique attributes that you can offer within this industry?

You will want to pick words or phrases that all have the same level of significance. You should also choose words that are relevant to your next position. So ask yourself which attributes from your brainstorming list define you best? What search words might members of your audience use if they were trying to Google the right candidate or person? What characteristics are unique to someone in your role? Once you choose words that highlight your areas of expertise and special characteristics, you then need to validate their importance to your audience. These key words not only differentiate you from others but also align you with your target audience. Ultimately, these words, when taken together with your heading information, should give your audience a clear understanding of who you are without reading further.

The key word section may not be appropriate for all applications. In such cases, your key words and headline can be incorporated into the text.

The following pages list examples of effective key word groupings.

Sample Headings and Key Words—One Line

Partner
Herron and Boles Consulting
Strategic Restructuring — Large-Scale Cost Reduction — Post-Merger Integration

---

Member of Technical Staff
Massachusetts Research Corporation
Program Management — DSP Chip Validation — Emulation System Design

---

Corporate Controller
McHenry Corporation
Food Service — Supply Chain — Inventory Control — Scorecard — Big Four Experience

Individuals in Transition, No Current Company

Process Engineer
Business Planning — Global Project Management — Creative Solutions

---

Wireless Product Marketing Director
Product Management — MVNO — Pricing — Billing — Customer Care

---

Global Sales and Marketing Director
Cross-Cultural — Growth Strategies — Fluent in Spanish — Commercial Real Estate

---

Sample Headings and Key Words—Two Lines

There are a few situations where a second line of key words is useful, but this format should not be used indiscriminately. We recommend the two-line format with only 10% to 15% of our clients.

In some situations, you may want to highlight two distinctly different sets of qualifications so that your reader will be able to fully appreciate your capabilities and experience. In other words, the two-line format should only be used when two lines are needed to provide someone with a complete picture.

The main line includes the key words that essentially define you. The second line of key words will normally provide one of the following:

- Specific expertise showing the breadth of your functional capabilities
- Selected in-demand technical expertise
- Breadth of industry experience

We recommend that you not use a second line unless there is a compelling need to do so. It has the potential of diluting the focus on your key attributes and thus could reduce the impact of your bio. Here are some examples of key words where two lines are appropriate.

Individuals Currently Employed

Director of Development and Quality Assurance
Smart Systems Inc.

Systems Development — Quality — CMM — Global Support Services
Web-enabled — n-Tier — Wireless

District Manager, Southeast Region
ARZ Computing

Consistent Top Performer — Quick Learner — Entrepreneur — MBA
Sales — Sales & Account Management — Professional Services — Product Management

---

CEO and President
Spindle, Inc.

Vision — Growth — Business Restructuring — M&A
Market Expansion — New Product Development — Complex Sales — Outsourcing

---

Individuals in Transition, No Current Company

President — General Manager — Senior Executive

Fortune 100 — Startup — Growth — Multinational
Business Transformation — Operations — Finance — Change Management

Other Tips for Key Words

Order: Once you have selected your key words, you need to make sure that they are presented in logical order. Start by making sure that related words go together. Don't mix and mingle. The most important word or phrase goes first, and the second most important usually goes last. The less important words and phrases go in the middle. Ultimately, the words should flow and make good sense.

Shortest Form: You will want each key word to be the shortest form of the word that is still plainly recognizable to your readers. Acronyms like CPA, MBA, HTML, CRM are all common enough so that you probably do not need to spell them out and waste valuable space in your key word line.

In other cases, the use of acronyms may depend on your target audience. You can play with the words and abbreviations to get maximum impact in the limited space available. Consider a logistics professional who wants to communicate her expertise in Supply Chain Management. She could use any of the following, depending on her target readers: Supply Chain Management, Supply Chain, or SCM. If most of the readers in her target audience understand SCM, then that's the best choice. But don't take it for granted. And, if you are concerned that some readers might not understand, you always have the option of spelling out these acronyms in the body of your bio.

Paragraph 1: Positioning

As previously mentioned, the positioning paragraph is a reformatted version of your written Personal Introduction. Take your written introduction, change it to third person and then convert it to full sentences. Use your full name to start and then use either your first or last name for subsequent references. The use of your last name is a more formal approach.

Here are some examples of good first sentences for your positioning paragraph.

- Samuel Smith is an entrepreneurial CEO and business leader with outstanding technology sales background and performance records.

- Baheera Khalid is a leader in understanding and addressing "make or break" issues at the intersection of business and technology.

- Andrew Anton is a business-savvy human resources executive with extensive background in compensation, benefits, and training.

- Rachel Robbins is a proven general manager with a keen understanding of financing strategies, markets, and people.

- Raj Patel is a petrochemical engineering manager with experience in planning and designing major capital projects.

- Pamela Walton is a turnaround executive who builds sustainable and profitable businesses through disciplined management and market expansion.

Make sure this description section properly reflects the level of power you have in your organization. Does this description differentiate you from newly minted MBAs, analysts, or associates with a year of experience? If not, you will want to "power up" your description to reflect your actual level of experience and the full range of your accomplishments.

Here are some great examples of powerful first lines.

Q: Do you know why proper bios are written in third person?

A: A bio has evolved as a shortened form of a biography—a literary genre where one person writes about the life of another.

- Keisha Martin is a pioneer in healthcare informatics.

- Laurie Wong is a consulting partner who has spent her career driving large global projects.

- Mark Samuels is an emerging market strategist with CEO and venture capital experience.

- Dr. David Smythe is an internationally respected scientist, entrepreneur, devoted educator, and research mentor.

Paragraph 2: Current or Most Recent Job

Starting with "Currently as . . ." or "Most recently as . . ." [your title], indicate the nature of the company's business and a summary of your responsibilities. Here's an example:

"Currently serving as Corporate Controller for American Industries, a publicly held global manufacturer and distributor of specialty materials, John manages all financial operations worldwide, including integration of all M&A initiatives."

The next sentence needs to summarize the most stunning accomplishment you've had in that job. What did you achieve that changed the company, changed the world, or rocketed you into stardom? This should not be your resume, nor should it be a chronology of your experience. Think of this sentence as the equivalent of a press release. You get to cherry pick the achievements you wish to highlight. A second sentence may be used to emphasize one additional significant accomplishment. In the entire bio, you will be able to talk about only two to three accomplishments, so make them count.

Depending on your career history with your current company, this paragraph can be about your most recent job, all jobs at this company, or the most important job you had at this company. The goal is to balance this paragraph with the next paragraph to highlight your experience in the right context.

Be Careful

Any sensitive corporate information—especially financial numbers, strategic programs, or company statistics that are not a matter of public record and that could influence the market or stock price of the company—should NOT be included in your bio. Your bio is not the place for Wall Street analysts to find out what your company is doing or planning to do. In most instances, you can use wording like "multi-million dollar" or other general descriptors to help tell your story. But you have to **carefully discriminate** between open disclosure and company information that should be kept confidential.

It may, for example, be necessary to name names. If you are or were in a job where you were responsible for important customers, you will be credentialed by the clients that you handled. If that is a matter of public record, you should consider using their names as part of your description.

For example, "Jose was the Major Account Executive for the Oil and Gas Industry. His accounts included Shell and Exxon." It would not be appropriate, however, to disclose the exact dollar amount of each account, nor is it really necessary. The scale and reputation of such companies speak for themselves.

If your most recent job was off track, not successful, or inconsistent with your future plans, you will want to say as little about it as possible. After mentioning that job, immediately focus on the next most recent job. Hopefully that will have been more interesting and more successful.

If you have had a series of "bad" jobs in the last few years, then you can merge them into a "topic". For example, "Over the last few years, John has held marketing positions at Company A, Company B, and Company C." Or "Over the last few years, John has held consulting positions with well respected boutique firms serving the high tech sector." Regardless of recent problems in your work history, you must have had some "wow" events or accomplishments in your career. Talk about them.

Paragraph 3: Prior Experience

This is the place to sum up the rest of your career, all in one paragraph. We know that's a tall order. But it can be done and that's what you have to do. It's not as hard as you think. Before you start writing the third paragraph, consider what you want to say. The goal is to design a paragraph that flows from and works with the previous paragraph.

First, review your entire career and identify those "high impact" accomplishments that are aligned with the next job you want. Then, decide what message you want to deliver about your skills and contributions, consistent with your target job. Remember, this is an advertisement for you.

This paragraph often begins with either "Previously, . . ." or "Prior to . . ." Here's an example:

> *"Previously, John was Director of Marketing at Company Q where he led strategic marketing initiatives for global expansion. In this role, he positioned the company for the first U.S. entry into the Chinese widget market."*

This is the place to tell how you saved the world, saved the company, or were responsible for a major breakthrough. If you are an individual contributor and your accomplishments are measured more by the projects you are associated with than your personal work, you can credential yourself through the whole project. For example:

> *"Previously, Sally was a database designer with Company R. She participated on the team that brought the Challenger back to Earth."*

Here's another way:

> *"She was a critical contributor to the project that . . ."*

Some people may have a sequence like this:

> *"Earlier Margaret was a project manager with S Bank and led an international systems development team when the bank expanded its credit card business overseas."*

The last sentence of this paragraph will be a simple statement about the beginning of your career to complete the chronology. Yes, it is important to go all the way back to the beginning. But it is one simple sentence, not a paragraph. For example:

> *"Margaret began her career as a systems programmer with Company T."*

Paragraph 4: Credentials

For most people, education will be an essential part of this paragraph usually placed at the beginning or at the end. You may start the sentence this way: "Sam holds a BS in Biology from XYZ University." If you have multiple degrees, it becomes a list: "Jane holds a BS in Accounting from ABC University and an MS in Taxation from PQR University." It is customary and permissible to use the shorthand designations—BS, BA, MBA, etc. However, if your degree is somewhat uncommon or not readily known to your audience, you may want to spell it out completely. A BFA is a Bachelor of Fine Arts. Surprisingly, there are several different "MM" degrees: Master of Mathematics, Master of Music, Master of Molecular Medicine, and Master of Management, for starters. Degrees from other countries are often named differently and should be spelled out along with the domestic equivalent for comparison purposes.

If you don't have a degree but are college educated, you may say that you "received your education at GGG University". If you have not attended college or took only a few hours of classes, then just leave it out. Emphasize your other credentials.

This paragraph also includes any other relevant and meaningful credentials. Do you have any of the following?

- ❑ Certifications: CPA, PMP, CFA, CFP, CFM, PCC, LCSW, or one of the multitude of others

- ❑ Awards—Internal: President's Club, Leadership Award, Top Salesperson

- ❑ Awards—External: Small Business of the Year, Most Valuable Volunteer

- ❑ Languages: Spanish, Chinese, Italian (Fluent? Conversational? Has working knowledge of?)

- ❑ Publications: Articles, Books, authored or quoted in

- ❑ Speaking Engagements: Workshops, Keynote Addresses, Panelist

- ❑ Leadership or Memberships: Civic Organizations, Industry Organizations, Charitable Organizations (Do you have "wow" accomplishments with any of these?)

Faith-based Affiliations

If your community involvement is in faith-based organizations, you need to be careful how you present the information, if at all. This decision is purely personal and will depend on both the circumstances and your audience. It may be completely appropriate in some situations and inappropriate in others. Tread carefully and judiciously.

Hobbies

If you have hobbies in which you have a level of leadership or achievement that reflects appropriately on your professional stature, then you should include them. For example, "Harry was the Captain of the U.S. Olympic Equestrian Team." That shows both leadership and an impressive level of dedication and achievement. Riding the trails on weekends doesn't.

Things to Leave Out

In a professional bio, it is not appropriate to include your family, your age, your sexual preference, or your family's place in the social register. Here is an example of what should never appear in a bio: "Joe married Sarah, his high school sweetheart, in 1991. They live in Rochester with their three children, John, Sally, and Henry. He enjoys golfing and boating."

Test Your Bio

Just like you did with your Personal Introduction, once you have written your bio, you should ask people for feedback. As we explained earlier in the book, if you request unstructured feedback (How do you like this? What do you think?), you will get "Looks good to me" or "It's fine." That is not helpful.

As before, if you give people specific guidelines for their evaluation, you will get information that will help you refine your bio and make sure that it is on target. You can use exactly the same questions and feedback form that you used earlier.

Remember, the more you test your bio, the better the end result.

The Final Test

- If you received this bio, would you be interested in meeting this person?
- Would you be willing to forward it to a colleague for an open position, a speaking engagement, or other consideration?
- Is this person someone who you would hire to provide the services you need for your company, your department, or your project?
- Are you excited about you?

Sample Bios

Included on the following pages are several sample Foundation Bios. We've tried to offer a broad selection so that you may see how the principles outlined in this book are applied for different people. Of course, as you create your bio, you have to add contact information, usually in a footer at the bottom of the page. Include at a minimum your physical mailing address, phone number and email address. Also, if you are using the bio in conjunction with your resume, keep the font and overall design consistent.

Roger Parmeet

President and CEO
Evernet International Group

New Markets — Global e-Commerce

Roger Parmeet is a successful technology startup executive, holding various CEO and general management roles. He has a proven track record in opening markets and creating traction for new products and services. Through his career, Roger has created valuable business strategies and provided personal leadership, resulting in profitable operations and partnerships in North America, Europe, and Asia/Pacific. As a speaker at industry events and contributor to articles and white papers, he is regarded as an expert on global e-commerce issues.

Since joining Evernet in 1999, Roger has led and transformed the company as Executive Vice President and now as President and CEO. Evernet is the global leader in e-commerce for digitally available products and services. While at Evernet, Roger launched subsidiary company International Digital Markets (IDD), the world leader in distribution for digital products. IDD supplied industry leaders such as books.com and Targon Micro.

Previously, Roger spent five years with software publisher Darkdisk as Vice President and General Manager. While at Darkdisk, he launched the successful DownloadProducts.com business and eventually sold it before joining Evernet.

Earlier in his career, Roger held management roles with electronic mail publisher N2 Software and marketing agency company Select Media Corporation. He also ran his own technology consulting firm after graduating with a BS in Finance from Texas A&M University.

Leslie J. Barton
Vice-President and General Manager, International
ipNet, Inc.

High Tech — Global Marketing — Branding

Leslie Barton has an impressive track record of architecting and building profitable technology businesses through growth phases and beyond at ipNet, Dellgate and Sunpaq after founding and building a successful software company. She is recognized for leading high performance teams worldwide that penetrate markets, build brands, and deliver deals that provide business resiliency, even in adverse economic conditions. Throughout her career, Leslie has provided general management and marketing leadership in the hardware, software and telecommunications industries.

Currently, as Vice President and General Manager, International, for a leading global media-over-ip company, Leslie heads all ipNet concerns in the Pacific Rim and Eastern Europe. Since joining ipNet in 1998, Leslie spearheaded the transformation of the company's Systems Division sales strategy resulting in exponential increases in both the size and number of deals with the top 100 telecommunications and media companies.

Previously, Leslie spent six years in the hardware business at Sunpaq and Dellgate as Director and General Manager for various business units. While at Sunpaq she launched several international subsidiaries and was a founding executive member of Sunpaq's Internet Division overseeing strategy, marketing and sales for Sunpaq's Internet efforts. Leslie earned industry accolades for Sunpaq as Company of the Year and best worldwide ad campaign for the Systems category. She was also a member of the Sunpaq Worldwide Brand Committee. Earlier in her career Leslie founded and directed her own software company that later was sold to a German conglomerate.

Leslie holds BS and MS degrees from the University of California, is fluent in English, German and Japanese and is the author of two books and several articles.

Martin V. Long

Vice President, Services Marketing
Unified Logistics, Inc.

Service/Product P&L — Marcom — Outsourced Operations

Martin Long is a service and product marketing and management executive with extensive experience in third-party logistics marketing. Over seventeen years and three different companies, he developed and marketed bundled logistics services and products. Martin has an unswerving record of solving business problems proactively as well as responding to crises in real-time by quickly identifying the root causes and implementing a solution.

In Martin's current position, he is responsible for services marketing and management of the U.S. ground transportation portfolio for $1.3 billion global logistics company. In this role, he led the team that brought the trucking product line to profitability by increasing gross margin by more than 30% and reducing the cost of acquisition by more than 50%.

Previously at Dominion Trucking, which was acquired by Unified in 2002, Martin held the positions of SVP of North America Services Marketing and VP of U.S. Services Marketing. In these positions, Mike had P&L responsibility for the $500 million refrigerated hauling services for both the U.S. and Canadian markets. During this time, Mike managed the launch of a farm-to-market discount program that achieved a $25 million annual run-rate in its first year. Prior to Dominion, Martin spent 13 years at Richland Transportation in various product and services marketing positions.

Martin is a member of the Direct Selling Association (DSA) and holds a BS in Business Administration from Canton College.

Andrew M. Goldstein
Director, Benefits
Enviropower
Outsourcing — Occupational Safety — Disability Management

Andrew Goldstein is a business-savvy human resources executive with extensive background in compensation, benefits and training. In addition to his corporate experience, he has played key roles in startup subsidiaries in Europe and Latin America. He has special expertise in planning for people issues that accompany mergers and acquisitions. Andrew is recognized for exceptional program management and consultative skills that deliver high impact results.

Most recently at Enviropower, Andrew was assigned to the Puerto Rico Electric Power Company in San Juan, where he was responsible for Benefits, Occupational Safety, and Environmental Compliance. In this assignment, he led negotiations with vendors resulting in maintaining health plan benefits while limiting 2007 cost increases to 3.5 percent above 2006 costs, substantially below average corporate increases of 8 to 12 percent.

Previously at Enviropower, he held several leadership roles in Compensation and Benefits, as well as serving as HR Business Partner for the 1500 employee Customer Service division. Earlier in his career, he designed quality improvement processes that contributed to Enviropower's successful pursuit of the prestigious B.C. Case Quality Award. Andrew began his career in education, where he rose to the position of principal at a middle school near Phoenix, Arizona.

Andrew has been recognized many times for distinguished performance at Enviropower, including HR Director of the Year and the Chairman's Leadership Award. He is active in the Society of Human Resource Management (SHRM) and World@Work (formerly American Compensation Association). Andrew holds a BS from the University of Wisconsin and an EdD from Arizona State University.

Shana H. Milner

Vice President, Supply Chain
Med Supply Corporation

Global Business Strategy — Finance — Enterprise Systems

Shana Milner is a proven strategy executive with strong financial and information systems leadership experience. She quickly grasps a company's vision, develops strategic options for successful implementation, and facilitates collaboration among stakeholders. She finds hidden value in business opportunities. Shana is trusted to lead large, complex initiatives requiring successful behavioral change. She is known as a thought leader in global supply chain.

Currently, as Vice President Supply Chain for Med Supply, the leading $30 billion hospital and medical supply distributor, Shana is the program officer and chief architect for the multi-million dollar National Supply Chain Project. The project is driving the creation of a new supply chain business model and is one of the largest, most complex projects ever undertaken by the company. This initiative is regularly cited by Med Supply's CEO to the analyst community as having been central to the on-going increase in corporate profitability and in creating sustainable competitive advantage.

Previously at Med Supply, Shana served as the program director of the now fully implemented Corporate ERP Solution project. Earlier Shana held financial positions with Med Supply including the Director of Operations Review, reporting to the Chairman of the Audit Committee of the Board of Directors. She also served as CFO of Med Supply's Surgical Specialty Division. Shana started her career on the accounting staff of Altics Manufacturing Company.

Shana represents the medical supply industry on the prestigious Global Supply Chain Roundtable alongside other recognized leaders in their respective industries. Shana is a CPA and holds a BS in Accounting from Boston College.

Nichole Sherrod

Partner, Consumer Products
Bearing & Loitte

Lean Manufacturing — Outsourcing — Systems Integration

Nichole Sherrod is a respected Bearing & Loitte partner specializing in improving business process performance for the consumer products industry. She has spent the past several years criss-crossing the globe working in the manufacturing arena to advance factory floor processes. Nicole is counted on by clients to define critical issues and counsel their business leaders on ways to impact the success of their operations. She is recognized as a person who understands the business operations and technical side equally well. Her perspective comes from spending extensive time in plant locations with the client's employees.

In her current role, Nicole is responsible for managing a global program driving business results from "operational adaptability" platforms. She was instrumental in developing the innovative methodology that now in its 3rd release is generating broad interest in Bearing & Loitte's client base.

As a partner, Nicole has responsibility for mentoring and developing Bearing & Loitte's workforce. She currently plays a leadership role in the community of female executives across the Consumer Products practice. She was promoted to Partner in 1999 and is one of the few females in her peer group. Nichole joined Bearing & Loitte immediately following college graduation and rose rapidly to her current position. In previous years, she has led multiple deployments of MRP systems in more than 70 countries.

Nicole is a member of the Women's Network of Chicago, Illinois. She is currently working with the Herman H. Minton School of Management at Midwest University to develop a certification program in advanced manufacturing. She holds a BA in Economics from the University of Minnesota and an MBA from Staufield University.

Just to show you that a powerful bio can be created for anyone, we have taken information from the Internet about the M*A*S*H character Colonel Sherman Potter, played by actor Henry Morgan, and created his bio. Hopefully, you will immediately recognize him.

Colonel Sherman T. Potter, MD

Associate Medical Center Director
Harry S. Truman Memorial Veterans' Hospital
Columbia, Missouri

Decorated Wartime Field Officer
General Surgeon
Hospital Administrator

Colonel Sherman T. Potter is both an excellent surgeon and leader who is frequently called upon for his knowledge of wartime surgery. He leads mainly by example, always doing his best and encouraging other to do the same. While easygoing by nature, no one doubts his authority. He is direct and decisive when he needs to be. He is respected not only by his troops but by his peers and those up the ranks. He is recognized for his ability to balance the spirit of army regulations with the difficulties of life in a war zone. Potter is a man of integrity and able to make the tough calls when necessary.

Appointed Associate Medical Center Director in September 1954, Colonel Potter leads the organization, direction, and coordination of all administrative functions of the hospital, including acting as liaison with the Veterans' Benefits Regional Office. Prior to his appointment, he headed the MASH 4077th deployed to Korea. Under his command, this unit was consistently ranked among the top performing units during the Korean War. Edward R. Murrow, one of broadcasting's most illustrious journalists, covered the 4077th after returning from touring the Korean battlefields.

Previously, Potter completed medical school and served in various Army administrative roles after returning from active duty in France during World War I. He began his military career at a young age in the cavalry and continued his love of horses throughout his life.

Potter was a decorated numerous times during his career and proudly wears the Army Commendation Medal, Purple Heart, Army Good Conduct Medal, National Defense Service Medal, Korean Service Metal and the United Nations Service Medal. He served his medical residency in St. Louis and established his surgical practice in 1932.

Part Three

Bios in Business

CHAPTER 12

---

*T*HE FAMILY OF BIOS

Bios, bios, and more bios ... there are a wide variety of applications for your bio. They range from very short 50-word bios for seminar brochures to comprehensive credential heavy bios for Board of Director opportunities. While they are different in some meaningful ways, they can all be developed from your Foundation Bio.

The following charts give you a quick overview. Each one of these bios is described in more detail in the next chapters.

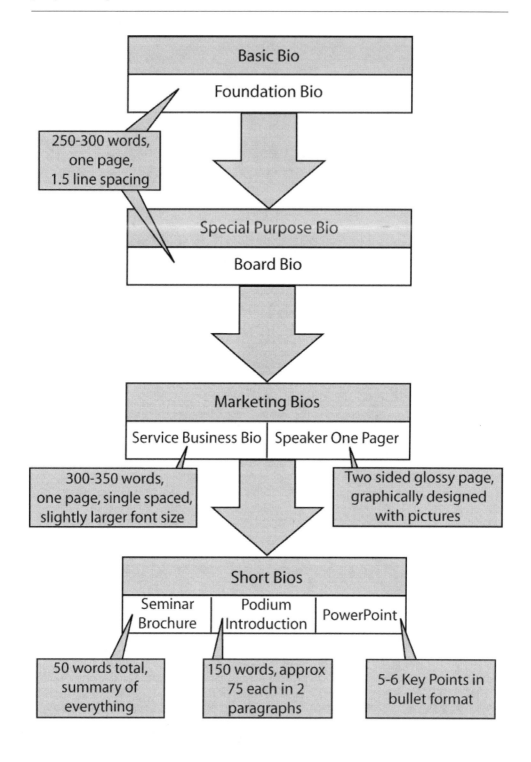

Foundation Bio

- Positioning Statement
- Current Job
- Rest of Jobs
- Credentials

Board Bio

- Positioning Statement
- Current Job
- Rest of Jobs
- Credentials
  Credentials that Qualify You for Board Membership are KEY

Service Business Bio

Key words
Services
Specialties

Customer Quotes

Positioning
Statement
1-2 paragraphs
Focus on Value
Proposition

All Jobs

Credentials

Speaker One-Pager

BOLD HEADLINE

Celebrity Pitch

Positioning
Statement &
Credentials

Programs

Testimonials

Client List

PowerPoint Presentation

- Statement
- Statement
- Statement
- Credential
- Credential

Seminar Brochure
Podium Introduction

Summary of Everything

CHAPTER 13

*B*IOS FOR JOB SEARCH

Since a professional bio is a key job search tool, most people will find that the Foundation Bio outlined earlier will also be perfect for their job search. These bios are typically distributed in one of three ways.

- Handed to someone in person

- Sent as an email attachment

- Embedded in the email body

While electronic communication and digital formats are increasingly mandated, there still are important occasions or situations when you need to have a hard copy document or a separate file that can produce a printed document.

Less Career Jeopardy

If you are currently employed, using a bio rather than a resume is a discreet way to provide potential employers with information.

Handed to Someone in Person

The statistics clearly show that the vast majority of jobs are obtained through networking. For networking with colleagues, friends, or friends of friends, a bio can be an invaluable tool. Although you will use your business cards at networking events, you will want to take your printed bio to any one-on-one meetings. Of course, the printed document should be professional, nicely formatted, and on quality paper.

In these private meetings, you want to share your background and objectives quickly so that you can focus on deeper levels of conversation. After the niceties, you might say: "John, thank you for meeting me. You might want to glance at my bio to get a sense of my background." The benefits of starting with a bio:

1. It will prevent you from spending your entire meeting talking about your history.
2. Properly written, it should engage your contact, making clear the contributions you can make.
3. It's one page, short, and has important information they need. That means people can keep it and pass it along to others, if appropriate.
4. If you are currently employed, the bio is a discreet way to provide potential employers with information.

Sent as an Email Attachment

As everyone knows, the days for mailing out printed cover letters, bios, and resumes are long gone. Electronic communication has streamlined the process, allowing people to convey important information quickly and efficiently. Even though many people don't open attachments, when there is a solid interest, there is often a need for an intact, standalone document that can be easily printed or uploaded into a database. Information embedded in an email is not compatible with most database applications.

Here are a few guidelines for getting maximum benefit from using email communication.

- Make the subject line of your email as provocative, relevant, and on-point as possible. You want to choose a subject that will make them want to open your email. For example, if you are following up on a lead from someone else, make the subject "Referred by Joe Smith", assuming Joe is a good friend or business associate of your recipient. If you know there is an open position, then you could put that in the subject line, such as "VP Sales Candidate".

- The body of your email is your cover letter.

- Be sure to include a complete "signature" that includes all your contact information. You may also want to provide specific times and dates when you will be most easily reachable.

Embedded in the Email Body

Many users of Outlook, which includes most corporate users, view their messages in a "Reading Pane" or "Preview Pane". The beginning text of the email shows up in the preview. By designing your email correspondence to take advantage of this preview pane, the reader will see your name, headline, key words and part of the first paragraph of your bio. Even when deleting an email, the reader is forced to see the beginning portion of your message. They can't avoid it.

To use this approach most effectively, here are a few additional guidelines.

- Craft your e-mail so that your bio text is divided into two parts. The first is a very brief paragraph that starts by that telling the reader in one or two sentences why you are writing. "John Jones suggested that I contact you directly about your open sales position ..." Add no more than 1-2 sentences aligning yourself with the position. Pick out one or two key requirements and indicate how you fit them. Close with one sentence indicating how you will follow up or any other action that is appropriate. Include your complete contact information below your name in the signature area, compressed into as few lines as possible.

> **Gotcha**
>
> Reading panes almost guarantee that your reader will see your message, even if they are deleting it.

- The shorter you keep your opening paragraphs, the more of your bio text will show in the Reading Pane.

- The second part of your email will be your bio, modified as follows:

  – Left justify the entire document

  – Convert to single spacing

  – Convert the Name font to **Arial bold 16 pt**.

  – Convert Title and Company font to **Arial bold 14 pt**.

  – Convert Key words to ***Arial bold italics 12 pt***.

  – Convert the body font of the text to 10 point Arial

- If you are working within a plain text message, you have very limited formatting options. Simply use ALL CAPS for the items that are bold. You can also use your spacing between lines to improve readability.

Following these guidelines, the transmittal email would contain the following.

From: John Mendoza
Date: Sunday, September 14, 2008 7:18 PM
To: Mary Baker
Subject: Referred by Sam Albright

Mary,

Sam Albright suggested I contact you about your VP Finance-Latin America position. I am an experienced global financial executive with considerable expertise in Mexican manufacturing. I lived in Mexico City for 2 years.

I look forward to talking with you. The best way to reach me is my cell phone – 555-999-9999. If we don't connect by Friday, I'll call you next week.

Regards,
John
4221 Marketplace Road, Milwaukee, WI 09999
444-555-1234 (home) – 444-666-9876 (cell) – john.mendoza@email.com

---

JOHN MENDOZA, CPA – BIO
Corporate Controller & Corporate Officer
American Corporation

Global Manufacturing–Strategy–M&A–Controls/Risk Management–Technology

John Mendoza is an innovative and strategic senior financial executive. He has extensive financial expertise in strategic investments and operational projects, primarily in the U.S. and Latin American markets. He is often called on to lead complex strategic initiatives to leverage a broad experience base, a consultative communication style, and a proven track record in managing project management skills. John has a unique capability to counsel operational teams to better focus operation and market strategies and to provide intuitive insight to the board of directors and executive management team to develop sound business and financial strategies. John is also integrally involved in determining investor communication strategy and managing the analyst call process.

Currently, as Corporate Controller and Corporate Officer for American Corporation, a publicly held global manufacturer and distributor of specialty materials, John manages all financial operations worldwide, including the financial aspects of M&A initiatives. In this role, he led the team that successfully established a $50 million manufacturing campus in Mexico – from Board approval through the start up. He also helped generate over $6.5 million in productivity gains by playing a key role in the successful launch of Six Sigma within the organization and by streamlining of consolidated reporting systems.

Previously, as Division Controller at Maximum Industries, he drove $1 million in savings from headcount reduction and system rationalizations in leading a reorganization of the finance team. He also served as a Senior Audit Manager where he reduced the audit budget over $500,000 by redirecting focus to business risk and developing more efficient audit tools. He began his career at GMPK International where he rose to the position of Audit Manager. While at GMPK, he spent two years in Mexico City, where he gained financial reporting expertise in Latin American business environments.

John is a CPA. He holds a BBA, Magna Cum Laude, from the University of South Florida and a MS in Accounting from the University of Florida.

Here's what John's email might look like in Mary Baker's Reading Pane.

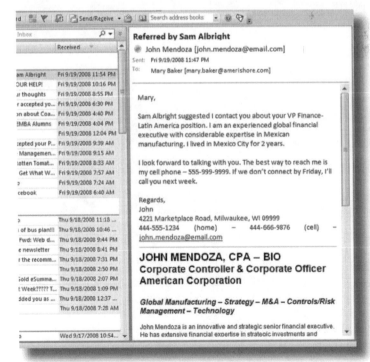

CHAPTER 14

$\mathcal{B}$IOS FOR MARKETING

Professional bios can be used in a variety of applications in the marketing and sales arena. As with all bios, a marketing or sales bio must address the needs of the audience, communicate the objective of the writer, and properly incorporate the purpose of the engagement. Discussed below are several of the more common applications for a bio in these settings. Many of these formats can be used interchangeably, depending on the amount of space available.

Business Proposals

A business proposal requires a special bio, particularly if you are in a consulting or service business. Customers are buying the expertise and problem-solving capabilities of the service team. It is often the most important factor affecting their decision. Customers need to be confident that they are buying unique skills and specialized knowledge that are relevant to their challenges. That means that your credentials, experience, and track record need to be presented in a compelling and targeted fashion.

The Business Proposal Bio can be submitted in two forms. A text format is presented in a written proposal and a bullet format is part of a PowerPoint presentation to the prospective customer.

The **text format** simply incorporates the "topic sentence" from each paragraph in your one-page bio. Of course, each sentence will need to be edited to create a meaningful statement with a smooth transition to the other sentences. The key here is to condense the most important statements from your bio into one well-constructed paragraph. Use compound sentences to blend together thoughts that may have consumed a full paragraph in your longer bio. Use descriptive phrases sparingly. This paragraph is more factual than other forms.

If you find that a longer bio is required as part of your business proposal, simply use your Foundation Bio.

The PowerPoint **bullet format** will include 5-6 points, ideally no longer than one line each. Keep the slide short and clean so that it is readable and easy to understand. The slide heading consists of your name and title on either one line or two. The bullets should provide:

- A short version of the "Who You Are" part of your bio. Select the most important words that describe you.

- Specific expertise or knowledge that you bring to the engagement.

- A broad based statement about your industry or leadership experience. It could be about the role you have played, years in a particular industry, or a particular position. Since you can also credential yourself by the company you have kept, this is a good place to drop well-recognized names that will impress your audience.

- Special credentials, such as certifications, awards, honors, or articles you have written for high profile publications. If appropriate, foreign language skills should be mentioned here. While you can use two bullets for this material, the general rule remains that less is more.

- Education

Here is an example of how you might structure your slide bio.

ANDREW M. GOLDSTEIN
Director, Benefits

- Experienced human resource executive
- Specialized in compensation, benefits, and training
- Start-ups in Europe and Latin America
- Leadership of M&A organization integration
- HR Director of the Year and Chairman's Leadership Award
- BS University of Wisconsin, MA California State University, EdD Arizona State University

Be willing to customize. You may need to modify your format to meet the needs of your audience. If this is an internal presentation, for example, you don't need to include your company name. Also, if this is a marketing presentation from your company to a potential customer, the company name is redundant. It's either on the slide, shown in the footer, or obvious somewhere else. If you are making an external presentation where other companies are involved, you will want to include your company name underneath your title.

Finally, if a group of bios are being included in a proposal, they should all be formatted consistently. Hopefully you will have an opportunity to direct or give input on the format of the bios. If you don't, you will have to modify your bio to be consistent with the others.

General Marketing Materials

The design and format of your materials will determine the bio that you should use. Make sure that you use the form that works best with your marketing message and mission.

Words are important, but they are only part of any marketing package. So take advantage of the opportunity to be graphically creative, making good use of color, pictures and an interesting layout. Headshots can be used effectively to accompany a text bio. Unless you have a unique purpose and sophisticated designer involved, however, you should only use headshots taken by a professional photographer.

Websites

All companies today have websites, and many include the bios of board members, corporate executives, or owners. Large companies also often have bios posted on their corporate Intranets. These bios are intended to enhance intra-company communications and cross-functional or cross-organizational resource utilization.

The need for a website bio will depend on the nature of the company's business. Most large, publicly traded corporations will include bios for all of their senior executives. These bios, usually created by the PR department, tend to focus on shareholder interests and business objectives. We think that the bios of Eli Lilly's executives stand out.

Deirdre P. Connelly

President, Lilly USA

Deirdre P. Connelly was named president of Lilly USA in June 2005. She is a member of the company's operations committee and senior management council.

In the fall of 2006, Connelly was recognized by Fortune magazine as one of the 50 most powerful women in business.

In 2008, she was appointed to the President's Commission on White House Fellowships. In this role, she will help select the White House Fellows, a prestigious annual program that fosters leadership and public service.

Before assuming the role of president, Connelly was senior vice president of human resources for Lilly. She had been vice president of human resources for pharmaceutical operations since May 2004.

Born in San Juan, Puerto Rico, Connelly received a bachelor's degree in economics and marketing from Lycoming College in Pennsylvania in 1983. She graduated from the Harvard University's Advanced Management Program in 2000.

Connelly joined Lilly in 1984 as a sales representative in San Juan. In 1985, she began a marketing associate role in San Juan. In 1989, she joined the international management development program at Lilly Corporate Center and later became a sales supervisor in Philadelphia, Pennsylvania. In 1990, she returned to San Juan as a diabetes product manager. In 1991, Connelly was named national sales manager for the Puerto Rico affiliate and, in 1992, she was named marketing and sales director for Puerto Rico. In 1993, she became director of sales and marketing for the Caribbean Basin Region, including Central America, Puerto Rico, and Caribbean Island countries. She was promoted to general manager for Eli Lilly Puerto Rico, S.A., in 1995.

Connelly returned to Indianapolis in 1997. From 1997 to 2001, she held the positions of regional sales director, executive director of global marketing for Evista®, and team leader for the Evista® product team and was promoted to leader of the woman's health business unit in the U.S. affiliate. In 2003, she became executive director of human resources for the U.S. affiliate.

Used with permission by Eli Lilly and Company

Some of the nice features include the clean, attractive graphic design, a quality professional headshot, an emphasis on her noteworthy accomplishments, and a succinct overview of her career. Further, on Lilly's website, all the executive management bios are consistently formatted and structured.

Another website bio we like is Jeff Crilley's. It's short and sweet and really makes the point with a solid marketing punch.

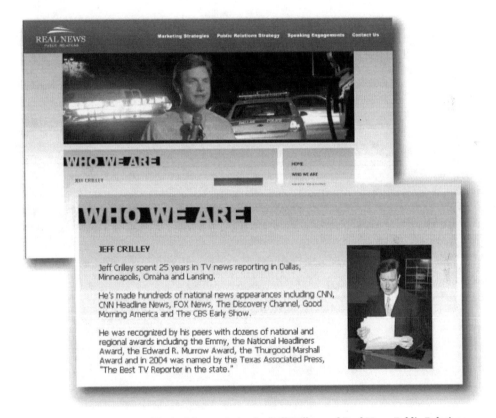

Used with permission by Jeff Crilley and Real News Public Relations

Remember: If you are an employee with a company whose PR department controls external publications, you need to be sure that any bio distributed to the public has been cleared through PR before it is released.

Small to medium-sized companies are more likely to include bios if they are service businesses. If a small company is selling widgets or generic services (e.g. carpet cleaning), they don't need bios. However, if a company is selling professional services, the expertise of its leaders and key staff members is important. These bios are part of a company's overall marketing. Thus, website bio pages should be creative, offering interesting layouts and engaging pictures. Customer testimonials can also be used effectively. We think Encore Management Company, Inc. has a website design that effectively presents its management team.

Used with permission by Encore Management Company, Inc.

Sample Website Management Team

PROPERTY MANAGEMENT   DUE DILIGENCE   CONSTRUCTION MANAGEMENT   REAL ESTATE CONSULTING

"Jackie has boundless energy, a proven record, and the ability to keep employees and owners over the long term. But most important to me is her integrity."

Daniel Allen
Insurance Broker

"I do not know of anyone with a greater commitment or desire to analyze and re-analyze her current operations and continually make improvements and changes as necessary to better accomplish mutually agreed upon goals, budgets, and objectives."

Larry Hudler
Investor

"Jackie's organizational skills are excellent and that is reflected in her well-trained staff."

Richard Morash
Investor

OUR TEAM

Jackie Jackson, President

Jackie Jackson is recognized for her savvy and business success in managing a wide-range of residential rental properties. With nearly 20 years experience in the residential real estate leasing and management industry, Jackie has expertise in property investment, consulting, and site management for conventional, HUD multi-family and non-profit rental properties. She is recognized as an effective leader, having built a well-oiled and loyal team of professionals who provide outstanding service to Encore's clients. Under her direction, Encore properties have consistently outperformed the market in occupancy and cash flow despite the challenging real estate market of the past few years.

Jackie treats every property as if she is the owner, maximizing resident satisfaction, owner cash flow and return on investment. She is an exceptional decision maker who gets into the details at the level necessary to make informed judgments. She maintains high occupancy rates and is able to turn around troubled properties. She has in-depth knowledge of the complex Section 8 housing market, including investment, site management, regulations, reporting and administrative policies. Jackie has expanded Encore's business, introduced the best practices in management, implemented new systems and developed sophisticated financial reporting and budgeting.

Prior to Encore, Jackie was Regional Vice President for The MBS Companies, where she increased portfolio NOI over 12%. Her North Central and Northeast region consisted of 41 properties totaling over 6500 units. Earlier, she was a Regional Manager with Property One, a division of Mutual of New York. She also held property management positions with Anterra Real Estate and Investment Corporation, J & J Consulting and Leisure Centers Inc./J&B Management Group.

Jackie is a National Apartment Association Certified Property Supervisor (CAPS), Certified Property Manager (CPM) and a HUD Certified Occupancy Specialist (COS). Jackie has completed numerous real estate management courses.

Encore Management Company, Inc.
2704 S. Cockrell Hill Rd., Suite B, Dallas, TX 75211
214-467-4900, info@encorecompany.com

Used with permission by Jackie Jackson and Encore Management Company, Inc.

CHAPTER 15

$\mathcal{B}$IOS FOR PUBLIC SPEAKING

Public speakers have to sell themselves as actors and performers—thus, their bios will reflect that. Accordingly, if you are a public speaker, you should have three basic bios.

- A very short form for inclusion in seminar brochures or marketing flyers

- A somewhat longer podium introduction to be used by the person introducing you

- A more comprehensive bio that is part of the speaker's "one-pager" used for marketing purposes by the agent or other person promoting your appearance

Very Short Form

The seminar brochure may be as short as 50 words. That's just two to three sentences. It should include your name, title, and company. It should also include the most relevant credential that would bring people to hear you speak on this topic.

Here's a good example:

David Dibble is Managing Partner of New Agreements Healthcare (NAH), a consulting and training company focused on creating sustainable change in healthcare. An in-depth systems thinker, he created the NAH System for Systems Thinking™ and NAH Systems-Improvement Tools™, a comprehensive set of process improvement tools. He has also authored four books, the latest on revolutionary results created in hospitals using the NAH methodology.

Used with permission by David Dibble

Podium Introduction

Your introducer will thank you for providing a well-written bio that he or she can read smoothly from the podium. It should be 125-150 words so that it can be read in 1 minute or less. A podium bio is structured as two paragraphs of equal length. The first paragraph is your positioning, with your key words incorporated into the text appropriately. The second paragraph is a summary of your career and your credentials. Remember, a good podium introduction is appreciated not only by the audience but also by presenters.

The bio reprinted on the next page is exactly as it appeared in the program for Houston's Association of Women in Computing Gala. Ann McMullan was honored as one of Houston's Top Women in Technology. Her bio was read from the podium as she received her award.

> **They Snooze, You Loose**
>
> A good podium introduction is short—1 minute or less! Time it.

ANN E. MCMULLAN
Executive Director, Educational Technology
Klein ISD

Ann McMullan is a broadly experienced educator who is leading the digital literacy revolution in schools by moving teachers and students from learning to use technology to using technology to learn. She is recognized as a visionary who communicates ideas, captures people's imagination, and moves them to action. Ann provided the leadership that resulted in Klein ISD receiving competitive technology integration grants totally over $1.5 million.

During her career as a classroom teacher, Ann earned Teacher of the Year recognition and was awarded the Leon Jaworski Award for Excellence in Civic Education. After advancing to district administration, she was named a finalist for State Technology Coordinator of the Year. Ann presents at major educational conferences and has authored several articles. She currently serves as co-chair of the state Educational Technology Advisory committee. Ann holds a BS from the University of Texas and an M.Ed. from Stephen F. Austin University.

Used with permission by Ann McMullan
and the Association of Women in Computing, Houston Chapter

Speaker "One-Pager"

If you are a professional speaker, you will need a sexy "one-pager" that highlights your range of topics, your credentials, and other special selling points. Key information from your Foundation Bio can be incorporated into this document, but it is a much more high-impact marketing piece than a simple bio. It is usually a two-sided glossy document much like a marketing flyer. Beyond your experience, credentials, and special expertise for speaking engagements, you will display your speaking topics with short descriptions, testimonials, and pictures.

If you are using an agent, you may need to adjust the bio to fit their format. You may also want to have your bio incorporated into special purpose marketing materials that can be distributed to your audience after a presentation. We think Brian Biro's one pager is a good example.

BRIAN BIRO
America's
BREAKTHROUGH
Coach

A Personal Message:

Picture all team members cheering for each other at the tops of their lungs. The unconditional support and energy is ASTONISHING! It's the last hour of a program that has implanted the most powerful principles of breakthrough leadership in every individual present. And now each individual has a magnificent WOO (Window of Opportunity) to breakthrough a self-imposed limit, fear, obstacle, habit, or doubt that has kept them from truly living with full, abundant, loving spirit. They face a one-inch thick wooden board representing that challenge. It is the moment to move from fear to freedom, from failure to faith. People who previously had difficulty working together, move from abrasive to embracive, from conditional to unconditional. By the time every single participant has broken through, the team has come together more closely than ever before.

In the months following the program, the organization has been ignited by reinforcing and building upon the foundational "vision keys" they received during the presentation. The result is a genuine "breakthrough" of tremendous proportion.

WHAT'S DIFFERENT ABOUT BRIAN BIRO?

ENERGY!
Brian Biro has the special ability to TRANSFER energy to the PARTICIPANTS! They come away dancing on the ceiling. Brian's events are flat-out FUN!

BALANCE!
Brian's principles, stories, and activities enable every single person in the audience to relate at a PERSONAL LEVEL. The result is a much more LASTING and ACTIVATING response to the programs.

HEART!
The final difference can best be summed up in one word: HEART! Brian's goal is not to make himself a star, but to help every participant KNOW that he or she is a star. In every seminar and keynote Brian has delivered participants love him because he is so REAL!

PROGRAMS

Beyond Success
This action-packed program moves the audience off the sidelines and into the game! All members of the team will become more connected to one another than you would believe possible in such a short time. Everyone will experience an unforgettable breakthrough experience and emerge with 10 powerful "Vision Keys" to carry into every aspect of their lives. This is a rich, involving and absolutely unforgettable experience for every person who attends!

The Unstoppable Spirit
Most companies and individuals see to survive in this world of accelerating change. In the Unstoppable Spirit presentation, you'll transform from mere survivor to ignited THRIVER. The stories in this special presentation will send your team soaring with new determination and new appreciation of their potential as they accept the power of personal responsibility, vision, and commitment to TEAM!

Breakthrough Leadership
Ultimately, no matter what industry you're involved in, you are in the BREAKTHROUGH business! Every day you seek to breakthrough with customers to generate loyalty, satisfaction, and relationship. The key to lasting success in business is breaking through with your own team members so they eagerly embrace personal responsibility, committed purpose, and leadership. This one-of-a-kind seminar experience ignites the energy and true leadership potential in every participant.

(All programs are offered as keynotes (90 min-2.5 hrs) or half-day (4 hrs) or full-day (interactive 8 hr. program) events. When offered as a half-day or full-day includes the Board Breaking Relay.)

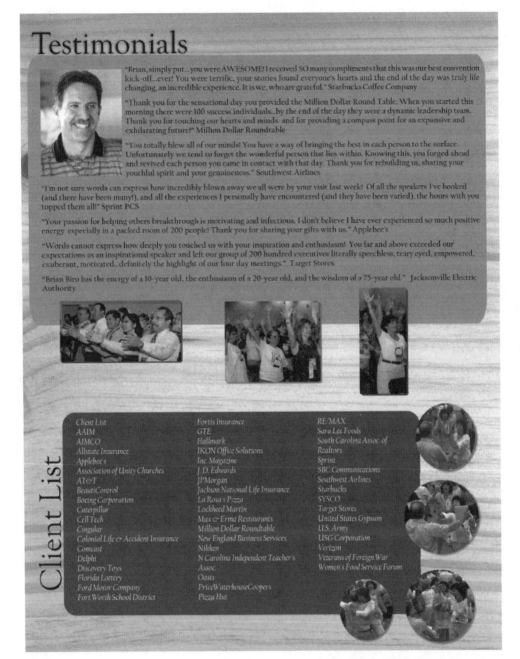

Testimonials

"Brian, simply put... you were AWESOME! I received SO many compliments that this was our best convention kick-off...ever! You were terrific, your stories found everyone's hearts and the end of the day was truly life changing, an incredible experience. It is we, who are grateful." Starbucks Coffee Company

"Thank you for the sensational day you provided the Million Dollar Round Table. When you started this morning there were 100 success individuals...by the end of the day they were a dynamic leadership team. Thank you for touching our hearts and minds and for providing a compass point for an expansive and exhilarating future!" Million Dollar Roundtable

"You totally blew all of our minds! You have a way of bringing the best in each person to the surface. Unfortunately we tend to forget the wonderful person that lies within. Knowing this, you forged ahead and revived each person you came in contact with that day. Thank you for rebuilding us, sharing your youthful spirit and your genuineness." Southwest Airlines

"I'm not sure words can express how incredibly blown away we all were by your visit last week! Of all the speakers I've booked (and there have been many!), and all the experiences I personally have encountered (and they have been varied), the hours with you topped them all!" Sprint PCS

"Your passion for helping others breakthrough is motivating and infectious. I don't believe I have ever experienced so much positive energy especially in a packed room of 200 people! Thank you for sharing your gifts with us." Applebee's

"Words cannot express how deeply you touched us with your inspiration and enthusiasm! You far and above exceeded our expectations as an inspirational speaker and left our group of 200 hundred executives literally speechless, teary eyed, empowered, exuberant, motivated...definitely the highlight of our four day meetings." Target Stores

"Brian Biro has the energy of a 10-year old, the enthusiasm of a 20-year old, and the wisdom of a 75-year old." Jacksonville Electric Authority

Client List

Client List	Fortis Insurance	RE/MAX
AAIM	GTE	Sara Lee Foods
AIMCO	Hallmark	South Carolina Assoc. of
Allstate Insurance	IKON Office Solutions	Realtors
Applebee's	Inc. Magazine	Sprint
Association of Unity Churches	J. D. Edwards	SBC Communications
AT&T	JPMorgan	Southwest Airlines
BeautiControl	Jackson National Life Insurance	Starbucks
Boeing Corporation	La Rosa's Pizza	SYSCO
Caterpillar	Lockheed Martin	Target Stores
Cell Tech	Max & Erma Restaurants	United States Gypsum
Cingular	Million Dollar Roundtable	U.S. Army
Colonial Life & Accident Insurance	New England Business Services	USG Corporation
Comcast	Nikken	Verizon
Delphi	N Carolina Independent Teacher's	Veterans of Foreign War
Discovery Toys	Assoc.	Women's Food Service Forum
Florida Lottery	Oasis	
Ford Motor Company	PriceWaterhouseCoopers	
Fort Worth School District	Pizza Hut	

Used with permission by Brian Biro

CHAPTER 16

$\mathcal{B}$IOS FOR PROSPECTIVE BOARD MEMBERS

Many successful executives aspire to sit on boards of directors in both the corporate and not-for-profit arenas. These board positions offer an opportunity to share expertise and give back to the community. They also provide a great network of high-level contacts and a way to differentiate yourself from your peers. In some cases, these positions can provide additional compensation and other benefits.

Boards generally seek people who can make substantive contributions to their organizations. They also favor people who have the standing and stature to make the organization stand out within the community, the industry, or the marketplace.

Expectations vary from organization to organization. Sometimes boards are seeking fundraisers. Others seek out people who can provide business advice and counsel. Still others will be looking for diversity or a recognizable brand name. To be a good prospective candidate, it is important to understand your target organization's expectations. You must be able to satisfy these requirements and effectively communicate that through your bio.

Networking is an essential part of being considered for a board seat. And bios are the essential tool for such networking. The bio used for this purpose, however, is somewhat unique. Since boards are looking for stature and pedigree, it is heavily focused on an individual's credentials. A board member bio has to deliver the strongest credentials, and they must be fully aligned with the organization. Everything about your background and experience, your customers, your awards, and your degrees needs to be presented with an eye towards credentialing.

In general, boards are looking for one or more of the following qualities in their board members.

- **Cachet**: Boards want their members to be well recognized so that they can bring an element of stardom and credibility to the company.

- **Functional Expertise**: On a board, it is important to have all business functions represented so that pragmatic and reasonable decisions are made. Boards usually include senior executives from a full range of functional backgrounds (e.g. Finance, Sales, Operations, Human Resources, Technology). This provides a board with a balanced perspective for decision-making.

- **Valuable Relationships**: Board members are expected to be able to open the right doors for their company. They are often selected because they know who to call and can effectively get things done through their networks.

- **Skilled Governance**: A company's strategic policy decisions are made by its board, with each board member contributing to the overall governance of the organization. The board is responsible for bringing thoughtful sophistication to the process of leadership.

In addition, not-for-profit organizations want board members who have a passion for their mission. They may also expect their board members to make personal monetary contributions in addition to helping the organization raise money from other sources.

The Board Bio

Using the same structure that you used for your Foundation Bio, you can write a new bio that is crafted for Board opportunities. A good graphic design of this bio, which may include a picture, improves your status. For a not-for-profit board, be sure to highlight your passion for the organization's mission and to include information about your ability to bring money into the organization.

Paragraph 1: Positioning Paragraph

Your positioning for this purpose should focus on what the board needs.

 Sentence one—Essence Factor: What is your professional essence from the perspective of being a board member? Who are you, viewed through the eyes of a board selection committee (and shareholders)? Remember, you may have to be approved by the shareholders. Why would this company want you on their board? What is the most important contribution you think you could make to this particular board? It might be your reputation as a "mover and shaker" within the industry. It might be your track record as a successful serial entrepreneur.

 Sentence two—Guru Factor: What special expertise can you provide? In what areas are you the expert? For example, you might be someone who has a knack for recognizing future technology trends. Another person might be especially astute in current compensation or legislative issues.

 Sentences three and four—Star Factor: What do you do? What have you done that has earned you recognition? Who has recognized you for your work? For example, you might be someone who has the unique ability to mediate conflicts. Or you might be someone who is recognized for your ability to listen intently to presentations and ask profound, provocative questions that guide the decision-making process.

Paragraph 2: Current or Most Recent Job

This paragraph will be similar to the one you wrote for your Foundation Bio. The question to ask yourself is whether the accomplishments that you have highlighted are the same ones you would select to present to the Board Selection Committee. Also, if you have high profile, prestigious customers who you have permission to disclose, you should consider including this information in the paragraph. They provide an additional form of credentialing.

Paragraph 3: Prior Experience

This paragraph will also be similar to the one you wrote for your Foundation Bio. However, it will be condensed as much as possible and only mention an accomplishment if it is directly relevant for this Board seat. By keeping it short, you leave more room in the last paragraph for your vast credentials.

Paragraph 4: Credentials

Boards like candidates who have already been discovered by other organizations. In other words, if you have been or currently serve as a board member, whether corporate or not-for-profit, then you really do have an advantage here. List it along with any leadership roles that you have held in industry, civic, or charitable institutions that demonstrate your ability to guide an organization beyond your current or prior positions.

Boards also like people who have been well recognized for their accomplishments, especially with awards or honors from outside their own company. Industry awards, civic honors or honorary degrees are examples of such credentials. Finally, you will want to emphasize any publications, speaking engagements, or other forms of external recognition. Just like in your Foundation Bio, you should include your foreign language skills as well as your certifications and degrees.

Sample Board Bios

ROBERT T. JOHNSTONE

Vice President & Practice Leader
Strategy and Organization
Able, Baker & Carter Consulting

Strategy — Transformation — Organization Design — M&A

Robert Johnstone is a master of installing growth discipline in organizations. He has a proven record of delivering sustained and profitable revenue, earnings growth, and shareholder value. He is recognized for finding new and hidden opportunities to create unique market positioning and strategic alliances. Robert is sought out for his expertise and insight and has served a number of companies, both public and private, as an advisory board member.

Currently, as head of the Strategy and Organization practice for Able, Baker & Carter Consulting, he delivered $5 million in annual gross bookings by developing and launching a new practice focused on integration of merged or acquired companies. He also led a two-year strategic project that resulted in $3 million initial contract revenues and an additional $10 million of revenue over the following 10 years. Robert has worked with clients including Dellgate, Walworld, and AXM.

Previously, Robert served as Senior Vice President, Corporate Development, at Micromeld Plc where he launched a $450 million venture fund. He has also held executive positions with PRG Electronics of Sweden and National Telecom.

Robert is member of the Sugarman University Alliance for Entrepreneurship and participates annually in judging the business plan competition sponsored by the MAT Forum. He frequently serves on industry panels and delivered the keynote address at the prestigious ARCA Venture Capital Conference this year. He was recently quoted in Business Month Magazine about making acquisitions pay off. His new book, *Organizational Transformation in Rapid Change*, was published in June. Robert serves on the Board of Directors of the Harmon County Boys and Girls Clubs. He holds a BS from Top Dog College and an MBA from Magna State University.

12 Technology Avenue, Cambridge, MA 02140
617-666-7777 Main • 617-668-9999 Direct • RTJohnstone@abcconsulting.com

Susan Salomon

500 Wilshire, Suite 40, Los Angeles, CA 90020
213.345.9876 • SusanS@AlphaMusic.com

President
Alpha Music, Inc.

Strategy & Vision — Shareholder Value — Turnarounds — Entertainment Industry

Susan Salomon makes dramatic business change and gets results. She is recognized for building successful companies and also for quickly recognizing when a company or strategy will not be able to achieve success and take appropriate action. Throughout her career, Susan has developed a rigorous approach to leading executive teams through the process of operationalizing a vision by combining experience-based knowledge with discipline and structure.

In her current position, Susan is President of Alpha Music, Inc., the $250 million publishing division of publicly traded Axelmann Worldwide, a leading global provider of entertainment services. She transformed the business model of this 75-year-old company and restored profitability by broadening the customer base and expanding its sources of revenue. Alpha Music is now recognized as the industry leader in classical music publishing in the United States and Europe. She also successfully completed a technology acquisition that increased shareholder value by more than $50 million.

Previously, Susan held executive positions at both MusicMakers and e-compose.com. She began her career in the entertainment practice of GMPK Consulting.

Susan holds a BFA from Simon College, an MFA from the University of Ridgecrest, and an MBA from Hunter University. Susan, an accomplished pianist and successful composer, has been an active leader in developing mentoring programs and performance opportunities for promising music students in Los Angeles high schools. She was recognized for her work by being named to the Music Publishers Hall of Fame. She has also been honored as Woman of the Year by the Association of Business Professionals. Susan has traveled throughout the world and is fluent in both German and Italian.

R. Harlan Martinson

Chairman & CEO
Fortune Foods, Inc.

Global Strategy — Market Leadership — Food & Beverage Industry

Harlan Martinson is as broad in his knowledge as he is in intense in keeping his $30 billion global organization on top, regardless of economic and consumer taste changes. His 20 years in the industry spanning worldwide markets, operations, and finance enables him to create far-reaching strategies that take into account the multitude of operational issues that make execution successful. He is known by all for his passionate commitment to health and wellness, diversity and inclusion, and values-based leadership. Those who work with him say he is unrelenting in his quest to "do things better."

Currently, as Chairman and CEO of Fortune Foods, Martinson led the company to a $10 billion increase in revenues, a 65% increase in net income, and an 80% increase in earnings per share over the past 5 years. The company's market capitalization surpassed $90 billion. Orchestrating the strategic acquisition of SportsPro Beverages early in his tenure as CEO provided Fortune with the momentum to enter the health and wellness sector.

Martinson has provided leadership in numerous positions since joining Fortune Foods, including President and COO, Fortune Foods; President, Snack Foods; and CEO, Mealtime Division. He also served as an officer in the U.S. Marine Corps where he achieved the rank of Captain.

Martinson is a graduate of the U.S. Naval Academy and received an MBA from the Darwell School of Eastern University. He is a member of the Board of Directors of Houston & Houston and a Trustee of the Darwell School. His community service includes serving as Chairman of the National Advisory Board for the Salvation Corps. He served as Chairman of the Corporate Board of Advisors of the Last Wish Foundation. Last year, Martinson served on the President's Council for Diversity in Consumer Marketing.

CHAPTER 17

BIO SUCCESS STORIES

Madison's Story: Bios Get the Job Done

Madison had completed a mission critical project for her current employer. Her subsequent job opportunities within the organization were not a good fit for her. She was a highly valued employee, but the only position that excited her required a move to Chicago. As a result, she decided to look for new opportunities. She worked diligently with her boss and colleagues to prepare the now-stable department for a new manager. When one colleague, Nancy, learned that Madison was leaving, Nancy insisted on introducing Madison to her prior employer, a major technology company based in town.

Nancy sent Madison's resume to about six people at her former company along with a personal note introducing Madison. After 2 weeks, there was no response. Madison then decided that she should send her bio to Nancy so that she could forward that to her contacts. Within two days of receiving Madison's bio and a second note from Nancy, the company contacted Madison to arrange a series of interviews.

Moral to the Story: Resumes don't always get the job done. They are not the best introductory piece. There is too much detail, which gets in the way of telling a compelling story. Bios work. They are more exciting, easier to read, and more effective in generating interest.

Enrico's Story: Telling Your Story in a Bio

Enrico's boss shared with him the company's new organizational structure in which the boss was now responsible for Enrico's organization. As a result, Enrico was out of a job. Oops! The genesis of the shift came from the strategic redesign of the company's product line and operations that Enrico led. While not surprised by this turn of events, Enrico found he was hesitant to pursue another full time executive position. In each of his last four jobs he had reengineered or turned around four companies, and in doing so had eliminated his own job. His real talent, it seemed, was working himself out of jobs.

The direction he decided to pursue was that of a Turnaround Consultant. Within a month of creating his new business, he was invited to speak at the local Turnaround Management Association. In preparation for the event and to provide marketing materials both for the event and for his business, he worked with a coach to create a series of bios. In the first meeting, he told his coach, "I just don't know how to introduce myself. I just got fired. And I have been fired from the last five jobs that I had. I don't feel comfortable bragging about myself, and I don't want to stand up and just say that I've had 5 jobs in 5 years."

The coach was able to help Enrico reframe his experiences and unique abilities into a great story about his successes. The introduction from the podium during the event was one of the best moments of the evening. At the beginning of his introduction the program chairman stated: "I'm pleased tonight to introduce our guest speaker, Enrico Gonzalez, President of EDGe Consulting. Enrico has the unique distinction of having been fired by his employer in five of his last jobs. The good news about those circumstances is that every one of those companies are now more successful than ever because of Enrico's leadership and strategic vision. . . ."

Moral to the Story: Your bio is your personal press release. It's the most effective tool for "telling **your** story". No matter what your situation, you can leverage unusual circumstances to make your bio memorable.

Part Four

Practical and Powerful Applications

CHAPTER 18

*Y*OUR WEB PRESENCE

The Personal URL World: Positioning with Punch

People are increasingly using personal websites as an additional tool for marketing themselves. To do it well, however, you must stay current with technology as it changes and improves. And you must update the content regularly. If you don't, you will not only waste the opportunity to prove that you are "cutting edge," but will actually make yourself seem dated. A fresh, well designed, and well executed website can be a highly effective marketing tool. However, it doesn't replace other forms of contact.

Your website can be used to differentiate you from other candidates, demonstrate the fact that you are technology savvy, and provide a showcase for non-standard presentations such as abstracts, samples, deal sheets, videos and creative portfolios. Moreover, a personal website is useful in creating visibility now that recruiters commonly search the Internet for candidates.

> **No Cyber Bullet**
>
> A personal website is useful in creating visibility now that recruiters commonly search the Internet for candidates. It can be a highly effective supplemental marketing tool. However, it doesn't replace other forms of contact.

You must, however, have a well-designed site that appropriately reflects your personality and professional image. This is not a project to slap together. Either do it well or don't do it. All aspects of your website—from graphics to content—should be designed to present you as a professional. Remember, if someone finds you through your website, it creates their first impression of you. That means you must consider all of the factors we previously discussed about making a good first impression.

Getting professional help to design and develop your website has some distinct advantages. A professional web designer will know not only how to make it look good but will also be able to "optimize" your site for the common search engines (Google, Yahoo, for example). This is important so that people will be able to find you. Search engine optimization (SEO) includes, among other things, making sure that you have the right key words and page organization to get maximum visibility when someone is conducting an Internet search. If the site is designed using your name as the domain name, it has the added advantage of providing a personal email address: Mary@MaryParker.com or JP@JohnPowers.com.

Some people are in a field where a portfolio is virtually mandatory. A personal website is then essential, providing an excellent way to present relevant information to a prospective employer. For example, creative professionals, attorneys, investment bankers, musicians, artists and journalists can use their personal websites to display a broad range of their work by including videos, photo slide shows, deal abstracts, article clippings, and audio clips.

The LinkedIn World: Professional Connections

An interesting dimension in the job market today is the extent to which companies and recruiters are using Google searches and Internet-based social networking sites such as LinkedIn, Plaxo Premium, and ZoomInfo to find candidates. In addition, once a candidate has been identified, these sources provide significant intelligence about the person during the due diligence process. Thanks to the ubiquitous Internet, the details of our lives have become easy to access, and it's getting easier all the time. As such, it is important to understand how these networking sites work and how you can use them to your advantage.

These sites change form almost on a daily basis, thus no book can provide you with up-to-date guidance on how to navigate them. The key to using these sites effectively is to understand that they are ever changing, and you must continually explore the possibilities to make full use of these resources.

The greatest benefit of these sites—whether it's the now trendy LinkedIn, the up and coming Ning or the new site that will show up tomorrow—is that they allow you to stay in touch with your established network, make new connections and then reinforce those relationships. In today's world of career "free agency", individuals, not their employers, are in charge of their careers. Such tools facilitate people's ability to exponentially expand their networks.

Some of these sites allow you to obtain and manage your recommendations, displaying them in a publicly visible and easily accessible way. You can then link these recommendations to your resume, bio, personal website or a proposal being sent to a prospective customer. This is yet another way to enhance your image without seeming to brag about yourself. Here are a few sites that are in vogue as we are writing this book.

LinkedIn (linkedin.com) is currently the most popular and best known networking site for business professionals.

Plaxo (plaxo.com) is a free service that updates your address book automatically and syncs with several contact databases, including Microsoft Outlook. It is evolving into a more useful networking tool.

ZoomInfo (zoominfo.com) is a site that collects and organizes information from the Internet and makes it available with comprehensive third-party reviewed profiles. It offers premium services frequently used by recruiters.

ExecuNet (execunet.com) is a large global networking and referral organization for executives earning over $150,000. Among other things, it allows members to put their profile in front of executive level recruiters.

Ning (ning.com) is a rapidly expanding site where individuals or groups can create their own private social networks.

Increasingly traditional networking organizations for business professionals and job searchers are making the leap to the Internet, offering a variety of on-line services to keep their membership connected. They range from your alma mater's alumni organization to industry specific professional organizations.

This is just the beginning. As you start to position yourself in your market, remember that such Internet tools will continue to expand and evolve. You can use your existing network to find out not only where you need to be visible, but also to stay abreast of the new Internet tools and connections as they are introduced.

Once you find the appropriate sites, remember to use everything you've already learned from this book to craft your profile. This is the place to make sure that you have emphasized your Essence Factor, Guru Factor and Star Factor. Your profile needs to showcase your accomplishments, and it needs to underscore your credentials. A good professional headshot is also a plus. Your goal as you create your profile is to establish yourself as a person who is not only talented and capable, but who has the ability to make a positive impact.

The Facebook World: Global Social Networking

To understand just how fast technology is rewriting the rules of networking within the business world, consider the story of FaceBook (facebook.com). Founded by Mark Zuckerberg on February 4, 2004 to electronically connect his fellow Harvard students, it was first rolled out to colleges, then schools and companies, and eventually to the rest of the world. Today, it is the leading social networking site.

As of October 2008, FaceBook had more than 100 million active users with more than 150,000 new users signing up daily. According to Alexa's Global Top 500 Sites based on web traffic as of this writing, it is the 5th most-trafficked website in the world following Yahoo, Google, YouTube, and Windows Live! What makes Facebook unique is its ability to handle not just the written word, but also photos, videos, music and other shared links. Over 14 million photos are uploaded daily. Once the domain of the hip and young, it is increasingly being used by professionals and executives who want to connect more broadly.

Visibility Issues: Be Your Own Investigator

Do you know what is out there about you? What comes up when you "Google" yourself? The Internet and your web presence is a double-edged sword. You need to be visible and need to be found by recruiters, but you also have to be careful that what they find presents you in a favorable light. Internet searches have become a routine part of every employer's sourcing and due diligence process.

> Diligently monitor the Internet for what others post about you.

People have been removed from consideration for a job because of what pops up in an Internet search. The problem has become so significant that ExecuNet now produces an annual white paper entitled "Dealing with Your Digital Dirt".

It would be simplistic, however, to say "be careful what you post". That goes without saying. The real danger is that others can use sophisticated graphics tools to create content about you and post it on their sites, even without your knowing it.   This includes anyone from a friend playing a practical joke to a disgruntled employee. The damage such misinformation can do is significant.

Our simple advice is this: Diligently monitor the Internet for what others post about you.

CHAPTER 19

SELF-CONFIDENCE COACHING TOOL

Are you a manager? Are you a professional life or executive coach? Are you a consultant? Do you ever work with clients who are lacking self-esteem or self-confidence? Do you work with people in career planning who have lost track of their key contributions or have never clearly articulated the value they bring to an organization? Have you worked with people who are down on themselves and can't seem to reclaim their power? If so, you don't have to be an expert career consultant to help someone write their bio.

Collaborating with someone to create a personal bio can be a powerful positive experience. It can provide your clients or employees an opportunity to develop a fresh perspective by talking with you about themselves in rich detail and in positive terms.

The first part of the process is to help your "client" create the opening paragraph, which also serves as their short personal introduction. Work with them to identify their Essence, Guru, and Star Factors as described earlier in this book. Brainstorm together, identifying everything they can think of that would fit into any of these categories. If your client or employee gets stuck, here are some questions you can ask to stimulate their creativity or memory.

- What are you known for?
- If you looked across all the jobs you have had, how are you defined?

- What positive comments were listed on your last performance appraisal?

- What good things do customers say about you?

- Why do people select you to work on their projects?

- What do your employees like about you?

- What good things have your bosses, peers, or colleagues said about you?

- How do your friends and family describe you?

- When someone calls you for information, what is it usually about?

- What are you the "go to" person for?

- What special interests or knowledge do you have?

Now that you have the brainstorming list, work with your client or employee to select the most distinguishing capabilities and qualities, the ones that showcase them best. Then you can help pull it together into a short paragraph that makes sense, is succinct, and flows smoothly.

The second step in this coaching process is to have the client list and discuss those accomplishments of which they are most proud. Start another brainstorming list. The point is to have the client acknowledge all those places where they have made a difference and the ways in which they were winners. For the bio, you will want to select the three or four most outstanding accomplishments.

The last step of this process is to enumerate their credentials. Start with education—what degrees do they have? In school, did they hold an officer or leadership position in a campus organization or team? Any special courses or certifications are also part of their credentials. Further, you should include any kind of award, publication, recognition, special honors, or unique characteristics, such as extensive travel or language proficiency. This section can also include significant volunteer activities, especially those involving leadership roles.

The end result is often a client or employee who will say, "Wow is that really me? That person is so impressive." As a coach, you will also have learned a great deal about your client. As a manager, you will have gained insight into motivating and developing your employee.

CHAPTER 20

$\mathcal{P}$ITCHING YOUR BUSINESS

Pitching your business is almost the same as pitching yourself. It's just a different perspective. The only important difference is that the message will be centered on the business. Yes, in some cases, you ARE the business. If you attend a business networking meeting, you will be expected to stand up and introduce your business, usually in 30-60 seconds. Can you do it? How memorable will your description be?

Let's apply the basic model for writing a good personal introduction to your business introduction. Listed below are some of the key questions to ask yourself as you focus on your business.

Your Business' Essence Factor

- What business are you in?

- What services and/or products does your business provide?

- What niche does your business serve?

Your Business' Guru Factor

- What specific expertise is your business best known for?

- Are there areas of knowledge that provide the foundation for serving clients?

Your Business' Star Factor

- What do you do that sets your business apart from your competitors?

- How does your business deliver value to its customers?

- What is your approach to doing business and serving your clients?

- What do your customers tell other people about how you do business?

- Why do your customers buy from you?

Sample Business Introduction

Here is an example of a business introduction for a real estate agency.

> **Real Estate Agency**
>
> I am Samantha Corke with R&R Realty. R&R Realty is the top rated agency focused on the luxury home market in the Park Cities and Preston Hollow in Dallas, Texas. Our firm consistently tops the lists of most prestigious and profitable firms in the Dallas/Fort Worth region. Our clients say that we have a in-depth knowledge of the properties in this market and know how to work well with a luxury homebuyer or seller. We also have resources for specialized financing for homes in the $2-$10 million range. Our firm sets the standard for service and creativity in managing sales or purchases of high-end homes. Check us out on the web at www.rrrealty.com.

Sample Business Bio

In any service industry, the customer is buying reputation, trust, experience, and specific credentials of key providers. By using a carefully crafted business bio, you can communicate these characteristics in the context of talking about your business and your role in the business. Creating a standardized design for the business bio allows the firm to produce individual bios that go together well in a larger marketing piece. Here is a good example of a business bio for a financial services firm.

Affilated With One Resource Group, a national brokerage office.

WHOLESALE BROKERAGE
LIFE, LTC, DI AND ANNUITIES

PROFESSIONAL INSURANCE RESOURCE
AGENTS, ATTORNEYS, FINANCIAL PLANNERS, CPA'S

CAROLYN E. O'BRIEN

Carolyn O'Brien specializes in helping clients and advisors to take the mystery and confusion out of insurance products and case design. Insurance agents, financial planners, CPA's, attorneys and clients rely on Carolyn for a broad range of financial products and services, from analyzing existing policies to case design for wealth creation and wealth transfer. Carolyn has respect and trust with many advisors and clients for her ability to simplify the process of acquiring insurance. With over 20 years of experience in the industry, she has experience in both retail sales and brokerage and offers both to advisors.

Carolyn's goal is to help advisors increase their productivity and have more time. Her affiliation with One Resource Group provides the back office and compensation available with a national brokerage office. The combination of her technical knowledge, experience and dedication to helping advisors and clients is unique in the industry.

Prior to CEO Advisor Resources, Carolyn was affiliated with CPS/AZ as Kersting Insurance Services, LLC. Earlier she was Regional Director for Manulife Financial working in the wirehouses focusing on high net worth clients and estate planning cases. She was also Brokerage Manager for Arizona for Principal Financial Group specializing in business insurance and disability income. She began her career as a Northwestern Mutual agent.

Carolyn is a member of many professional organizations including the Central Arizona Estate Planning Council, Society of Financial Service Professionals, Women in Financial Services, National Association of Insurance and Financial Advisors , and the Arizona Community Foundation. Carolyn has held Board positions in several of these organizations. Carolyn holds a BA from Arizona State University.

"I am an experienced successful agent who has aligned myself with Carolyn on those "tough cases". My production has increased significantly."

Tom in Phoenix
Insurance Broker

"Carolyn has been instrumental in helping us with the insurance side of our estate and business law practice."

Sara Vannucci
The Forakis Law Firm

"With Carolyn's help we added an insurance division to our firm. We are happy to introduce her to our clients."

Kristy Mukai Barnes
Mukai Greenlee & Co, PC

10645 N. Tatum Blvd Suite 200-503 Phoenix, AZ 85028
Phone: 602.626.8181 Fax: 602.926.0384 www.ceoadvisorresources.com
Securities offered through The Leaders Group, Inc.
Member FINRA/SIPC, 26 West Dry Creek Circle, Suite 575, Littleton, CO 80120 303-797-9080

Conclusion

Our goal in writing this book has been to provide you with important tools designed to help you present yourself effectively to others. If you follow our methodology and take advantage of our worksheets, chances are good that you will start to think about yourself differently. The process of crafting an introduction and creating a bio requires you to explore and articulate the full range of your talents and accomplishments. It is a remarkably effective way to focus on the positive and move forward. We are confident that the person you discover while going through that process will be stronger, better defined, and more dynamic than you realized.

So take the time to explore the process. It will help you define yourself both to yourself and to your audience, which might range from a potential employer or a new boss to a business associate or the local PTA. The next time you are asked to introduce yourself to others, you will be able to answer with confidence and panache.

We hope this book has given you a clear roadmap for setting yourself apart from others and successfully creating positive first impressions in a wide variety of settings.

ABOUT THE AUTHORS

Paula Asinof, Principal
Yellow Brick Path
www.yellowbrickpath.com

Paula Asinof is a broadly experienced career management executive, an authority on resumes, and founder of Yellow Brick Path, a career coaching and consulting firm. She has been a catalyst for accelerating or redirecting numerous careers by helping successful executives and professionals move up or move on to their next career opportunities. Clients appreciate the depth of her "real world" executive experience in major corporations, in career services, and in executive search.

Paula is distinguished by her ability to identify, leverage, and develop talent. Throughout her career, she has helped clients, peers, and subordinates recognize their unique capabilities and position themselves as "A" players. She has a contagious enthusiasm and passionate belief in people that inspires them to become prouder, stronger, and more valuable contributors to their organizations. She has also led innovative initiatives to build top performing organizations with staying power.

In addition to founding Yellow Brick Path, Paula is a co-founder of Coach Academy Texas, a cutting-edge coach training program. Her background includes ten years of executive search and serving as Director of Career Services for Sanford-Brown Institute where she received the President's Leadership Award. Earlier, Paula held leadership positions in Information Technology and Finance with GTE (now Verizon), Rand McNally, Brunswick, and the Midwest Stock Exchange. She began her career at Laventhol & Horwath CPAs.

Paula holds an MBA from The Wharton School, an MA from Columbia University, and a BA from Washington University. She is an NLP Practitioner, a Certified NLP Coach (NLPC), and a member of the International Coach Federation (ICF). She has served on the Boards of Big Brothers Big Sisters of North Texas/Dallas County and the Friends of the Katy Trail, an urban thoroughfare in Dallas. Her articles on career management have appeared in the business and local press.

Mina Brown, Founder and President

Positive Coaching Group
www.positivecoach.com
TurnKey Coaching Solutions
www.turnkeycoachingsolutions.com

Mina Brown is an experienced and insightful executive coach, career consultant, trainer and public speaker. As a former senior executive and CFO, she offers the powerful combination of successful business leadership experience coupled with intuition, unflinching candor, and well-honed communication abilities. Her clients describe her as "engaging, compassionate, challenging, and inspirational." Plus, she's just plain fun to work with.

Mina is widely recognized and sought-after for her focus on tangible business outcomes. She works primarily with executives, professionals, and management teams in areas of leadership, communications, conflict, team effectiveness, and career management. She is a Certified NLP Coach and has numerous certifications in diagnostic instruments, learning tools, and other models, including: Kolbe Index®, Lominger 360° Assessment®, Conflict

Lens®, and TDF Decision Styles Theory and Assessment Instrument®. Mina is a longstanding member of International Coach Federation (ICF), CoachVille and a Founding Member of the International Association of Coaches (IAC). She has been the National Career Transitions Coach for 6 Figure Jobs.com for many years.

For more than 25 years, Mina provided operational and financial leadership for large successful public corporations. In recent years, she has worked extensively with leaders in the following industries: technology, telecommunications, automotive, financial services, venture-backed start ups, consumer products, and real estate management.

In addition to Positive Coaching Group, Mina is a co-founder of two other firms: TurnKey Coaching Solutions, a global coaching program management and contract coach staffing company, and Coach Academy Texas, a cutting-edge coach training firm. Previously, Mina held senior executive positions with Aviall, Inc., both as Chief Financial Officer and as SVP & General Manager of its Aerospace Division. She also held corporate management positions with Ryder System and Amax, now a subsidiary of Freeport-McMoRan Copper & Gold Inc. Mina started her career with Price Waterhouse.

Mina holds an MBA from Vanderbilt University, a BBA in accounting with highest honors from Eastern Kentucky University, and a CPA.

An Invitation from the Authors

We'd love to hear from you, whether you want to share your experiences, request our availability for speaking engagements, offer comments about the book, engage us to work with you or your company, or order additional copies of this book.

We invite you to contact us in one of these three easy ways.

1. Send or fax us a copy of the following page: 972-733-4228.
2. Call either of us: Paula at 214-526-8690 or Mina at 972-733-9963
3. Reach us on the Internet: www.besharpbook.com.

Be Sharp   Comment and Book Order Form

Comments/Requests:

❑   I am interested in booking a speaking engagement.
❑   I am interested in engaging ❑ Paula ❑ Mina to work with me personally.
❑   I am interested in engaging the authors to work with my organization.

Name: _____

Mailing Address: _____

City: _____

State: _____ ZIP Code _____ Telephone (_____) _____

Email: _____

Number of books*: _____ @ $14.99 per book $ _____

Texas residents only, add 8.25% sales tax ($1.24 per book) $ _____

Shipping & handling: $4.95 for 3 or fewer; $7.95 for 4-6 books $ _____

                        TOTAL ORDER $ _____

*For larger quantities or non-US addresses, call for special pricing

❑ VISA   ❑ MasterCard   ❑ American Express   ❑ Discover

Name on Card: _____

Credit Card #: _____ Exp Date: _____ CVV _____

❑ Billing Address Same as Above

Billing Address: _____

City: _____ State: _____ ZIP: _____

_____   _____
Signature   Today's Date

Fax: 972-733-4228   Phone: Paula   214-526-8690
www.besharpbook.com   Mina   972-733-9963

Made in the USA